P9-CSA-561

AGE AIN'T NOTHING BUT A NUMBER

AGE AIN'T NOTHING BUT A NUMBER

Black Women Explore Midlife

EDITED BY CARLEEN BRICE

BEACON PRESS *Boston*

Public Library, New Brunswick, NJ

BEACON PRESS
25 Beacon Street
Boston, Massachusetts 02108-2892
www.beacon.org

Beacon Press books are published under the auspices of the
UNITARIAN UNIVERSALIST ASSOCIATION of CONGREGATIONS.

© 2003 by Carleen Brice *All rights reserved*
PRINTED IN THE UNITED STATES of AMERICA

07 06 05 04 03   8 7 6 5 4 3 2 1

Excerpt from "Little Gidding" in *Four Quartets* copyright 1942 by T. S. Eliot and renewed 1970 by Esme Valerie Eliot, reprinted by permission of Harcourt, Inc.

This book is printed on acid-free paper that meets the uncoated paper ANSI/NISO specifications for permanence as revised in 1992.

Text design by Isaac Tobin
Composition by Wilsted & Taylor Publishing Services

LIBRARY OF CONGRESS CATALOGING-IN-PUBLICATION DATA
Age ain't nothing but a number : Black women
explore midlife / edited by Carleen Brice.
p.   cm.
ISBN 0-8070-2823-1 (alk. paper)
1. American literature—African American authors.
2. African American women—Literary collections. 3. Middle aged women—
Literary collections. 4. American literature—Women authors. 5. Middle aged
women—United States. 6. Middle age—Literary collections. 7. Aging—Literary
collections. 8. Middle age—United States. 9. Aging—United States.
10. African American women.   I. Brice, Carleen, 1963–

PS509.N4A35 2003
810.8'09287'096073—dc21
2003001235

CONTENTS

2. New Bones
Health, Beauty, and Self-Image

3. Roots
Family and Friendship

4. In Search of Satisfaction
Romance and Sexuality

Introduction

To paraphrase the popular saying: "Aging happens." One day you realize the woman on the cover of the magazine you're reading could be your daughter. The hot honey on your favorite soap opera wasn't born when you graduated from high school. The "oldies" on the radio are songs you danced to in college. The cute guy making your latte calls you "ma'am." And you feel like one of your grandmother's lace doilies.

Welcome to midlife.

African American culture isn't as youth-focused as the predominant culture, and we black women pride ourselves on aging well (comparatively smooth complexions on elder faces being a benefit of our melanin-laden skin). However, we are not immune to the fears, doubts, and disillusionments that come with getting older. How could we be? We live in a society that equates youth with beauty and values beauty as a woman's most important asset, a society that stereotypes black women as sexual objects when we're young and views us as mother figures (mammies) when we age.

Yet despite anxiety and discrimination, who doesn't want to age? After all, getting older beats the alternative, especially for African American women—for whom making it to middle age (let alone old age) is a victory over stress, poverty, limited access to health care, and diseases that kill us at higher rates than white women even if we have money, education, and health insurance. Sometimes it seems there are so many forces conspiring against us that it comes to this: *if we are lucky*, aging happens. As Maya Angelou writes, "Mostly, what I have learned so far about aging, despite the creakiness of one's bones and the cragginess of one's once-silken skin, is this: do it. By all means, do it."

We *are* doing it. The life expectancy for black women has risen to 74.2 years. And we're doing it with confidence, joy, and style. With role models like Tina Turner, Patti LaBelle, Oprah Winfrey, B. Smith, Carol Mosley Braun, Iyanla Vanzant, Star Jones, Johnnetta Cole, Judith Jamison, Pam Grier, and that quintessential goddess of aging well, Lena Horne, leading the way, we are redefining aging.

Indeed, the definition of midlife depends on whom you ask. Some say it begins in the middle or late thirties, while others say not until a woman turns fifty should she be considered middle-aged. I believe, as with all passages, that there are phases of midlife. Women in early midlife (in their mid-to-late thirties and early forties) probably face different issues than women in the middle of midlife (about mid-forties to early fifties), who may have different concerns than women in later middle age (fifties to sixties).

However, each woman is unique and has her own specific opinions and feelings about and reactions to getting older. And just because a woman is a certain age doesn't mean we can assume we know what she might be dealing with. These days, middle-aged women may be newlyweds or new mothers, as well as grandmothers or widows. We may experience the empty-nest syndrome or the overflowing-nest syndrome as more adult children stay in or return to their parents' homes. We may navigate the field of Internet dating, travel the world, teach homeless people, take up pottery, or study international business.

In addition, the enormous number of aging baby boomers is forcing this country to acknowledge that turning forty or fifty or sixty doesn't mean the end of a woman's vitality or usefulness. So midlife in the twenty-first century isn't our mothers' or grandmothers' "change of life" but is a time of transformation: emotional, psychological, professional, and, of course, physical. A transformation—like all transitions—that can be difficult no matter how fortunate we are to reach it.

As I entered midlife, I experienced a somewhat rocky evolution from young to not-so-young. As a writer, I am a reader through and through and always turn to books for information and enlightenment. I discovered helpful works such as *Coming into Our Fullness: On Women Turning Forty*, by Cathleen Rountree; *New Passages*, by Gail Sheehy; and *Awakening at Midlife*, by Kathleen A. Brehony. They offered positive depictions of women for whom midlife was a period of personal growth and empowerment, but still I longed for insights from African American women, who faced yet another "ism" (ageism) simply by having the good fortune to keep living.

I turned to one of J. California Cooper's short story collections, *Some Love Some Pain Sometime*, and reread the stories of women who find love and happiness after they discover themselves. I read Lucille Clifton's poem "new bones" with a deepened perspective and came to see midlife as the "sun and honey time" she describes. Looking for additional writings on getting older by black women, I rediscovered wonderful poems, essays, short stories, and novels and found others that were new to me.

I decided to put my favorite pieces together and to invite other writers, some well known and some who weren't widely published, to submit their reflections on midlife. That's how *Age Ain't Nothing but a Number* came to be. This is the book I longed for when I began my midlife journey, and one that I hope will provide you with information, inspiration, and good company during your middle years.

Within these pages you will find essays, poetry, and fiction that discuss aging from black women's perspectives. You will encounter a variety of opinions on midlife: from Gloria Wade Gayles, who entreats us to dance while we age, to Alice Walker, who reminds us that melancholy and sadness are just as important to our growth as the "dancing times." From Elyse Singleton, who is cautious about revealing her age, to Trudier Harris-Lopez, who threw herself a ball—not a party, a *ball*—for her fiftieth birthday. From Patricia Raybon, whose essay begins with the sentence "Let's be pretty tonight," to Terri Sutton, whose essay asks the heartbreaking question "Am I Ugly?" In all, forty women share their midlife experiences, revelations, hopes, and ideas. Divided into four sections, this collection addresses relationships, health, spirituality, sexuality, careers, and other topics as they relate to midlife.

The first section, "A New Attitude," deals with personal and spiritual growth and the goals, dreams, regrets, and breakthroughs of midlife. Highlights include Jan Thomas's discussion of her decision to leave the corporate rat race and work for a nonprofit organization and poet S. Pearl Sharp's upbeat prescription for facing fifty without fear.

In Part Two, "New Bones," which covers health, self-image, and the physical changes commonly experienced at midlife, *Essence* magazine editorial director Susan L. Taylor urges us to guard our health and poet Colleen McElroy slyly blames her aching joints and hot flashes on aliens who have overtaken her body.

Part Three, "Roots," addresses relationships with friends and family, covering such issues as parenting, friendship, losing a loved one, infertility, and taking care of elderly parents. Here, writer Joan Hopewell-Hartgens takes us to a "homegirl reunion" and Miriam DeCosta-Willis describes the pain and honor of her last years with her dying husband.

In the final section, "In Search of Satisfaction," which deals with falling in love, getting married or remarried, and the "sexual prime of life," poet Opal Palmer Adisa offers hilarious advice on what to do when the hair "down there" turns gray and activist Gale Madyun reminds older women to practice safer sex.

These are only a few examples of the wonderful works you'll find inside these pages. *Age Ain't Nothing but a Number* was written by wise, honest, bold, and vivacious women. It features a chorus of voices lifted up to sing the truth about midlife. I hope you let the words of these most remarkable women be a beacon that lights the way through your midlife journey.

1

A New Attitude

Personal Growth and Spirituality

At every single moment, we are given the opportunity to choose our future.

— *Iyanla Vanzant*, The Value in the Valley

The end of child rearing, of marriage (through divorce or death), or of a job or career (through retirement) can provide middle-aged women more time to ponder life's big questions. Growing closer to the time we will leave this plane of existence makes us more prone to introspection. We begin to wonder more about the life beyond the one we know. We start to wonder even more about our souls and what we leave behind when we die. What will be our legacy? What has mattered to us? What part of the self endures past the death of the body? Even if we have explored such issues in our youth, they become more compelling as we get older.

As we age, we get some answers; probably not the ones we suspected when we were younger. For experience has taught us that the universe is much bigger than our own little world. That life is mysterious and unpredictable. That the questions may be more important than the answers; the journey more important than the destination.

Once we begin to see ourselves more clearly, we can determine what our purpose is. When we're young, we often don't know our purpose or trust ourselves to discover it. Or perhaps we're too busy surviving to discover what we have to offer to the world. But as we age, we strip away the layers of old habits and old ideas that keep us from identifying and acting on our calling. As we get older, we can free ourselves to pursue our mission and to act on it. Midlife becomes the time to live our purpose; to discover our true selves.

Can you feel it? Can you feel your body, mind, and heart telling you now is the time? Now is the time to find your authentic self. Even those who have lived brave, full, exciting lives still have new worlds to conquer, contributions to make. We may fret about gray hair, thickening waistlines, and various aches and pains, but did you ever think these conditions might be nature's way of signaling us that time is moving on? Perhaps hot flashes are symbols of a metaphysical flame burning inside, spurring us on to do what we need or want to do before it's too late. Perhaps wrinkles are God's way of telling us that our boldest dreams for ourselves are in danger of becoming "raisins in the sun." There is time to rescue your dreams from that sad fate. There is time to reach out and do what you want to do. To make a difference in the world. To find freedom. Now is the time. Can you feel it?

Who Says an Older Woman Shouldn't Dance?

GLORIA WADE GAYLES

The band was playing, and we were dancing—men with women, women with women, men alone, and women alone. Just dancing. Having a ball. I sat down to get my second wind, having danced continuously to three numbers, when I heard someone at a nearby table say, "Can you believe the way she is dressed?" I looked at the center floor and saw her whirling. She was in another world. What daring, I thought to myself, noticing for the first time that she was dressed in a black microminiskirt and in black semisheer tights. "That outfit is what the students wear," I heard the critic say. I said nothing. Instead, I bounded up from my table and bopped my way to the dance floor. I made my statement in my dance. I danced wildly, knowing that people might think I was competing with her when all along I was affirming her and myself.

Perhaps I dance because many of our mothers could not, or did not. Perhaps I dance because I am celebrating the liberation they did not experience, but wanted so desperately for their daughters. Perhaps I dance as a way of screaming against the dirges poor black women hear every day of their lives. Dirges are for death, not life. I want to live. I want to live as fully at fifty-plus, at sixty, and at seventy as I lived at twenty, thirty, and forty. I want to live and therefore I must dance. I dance, then, in spite of my age and because of my age.

I know I am no longer young because in my night dreams and day fantasies I am holding an infant nestled against sagging breasts that give the aroma of love, not milk. That I am ready and anxious to become a grandmother is the most joyous age-music to which I now dance.

I know I am no longer young because my day visions of tomorrow show junior faculty with whom I work at Spelman College directing programs, chairing departments, writing books, winning awards, and heading institutions. Such joy there is in witnessing their becoming! We should not put ourselves on a shelf when we reach a certain age, but we must make a way, prepare the way and clear the way, for younger women when their time arrives.

I know I am no longer young because my financial planning focuses on retirement, yes, but more on the future of my children and my grandchildren yet unborn. I want to leave them enough memories to last a lifetime and enough money to get them through difficult periods, which today's conservative politics suggest will surely come. I know I am older when I stand naked before my mirror and see my brown, older woman's body with discerning, non-rejecting eyes. I see my hands. As I move fast toward sixty, they are designed with a network of tiny lines. They are my hands, and with them I can hold myself and others.

I see my face. The lines around my mouth are deeper now than they were last year and the dark hollows beneath the eyes, a genetic trait, are darker. It is my face, and it wears the smile I give myself and others.

I see my neck. It asks for high-neck blouses and scarves that accentuate as they cover, but it rests on shoulders sturdy enough for my weight and the weight of others.

I am not depressed about being older, and yet sometimes it is my voice I hear when Nina Simone, in the deep dark chocolate of her alto, sings, "I live alone. . . . The walls talk back to me and they seem to say, 'Wasn't yesterday a better day?'" Sometimes yesterday haunts me. It is the train whistle I hear when a litany of regrets disturbs my sleep, or the train itself, grander, perhaps, than in reality, moving to places once filled with my breath and shaped by my desires. I want to board yesterday, so much do I miss the texture of the

6

life I lived then, the joys that are now then-joys. I miss yesterday, sometimes with an ache that defies description. If only I could relive my life, so much I would say and not say, feel and not feel, think and not think, do and not do, accept and reject, learn and unlearn, struggle to keep and find the courage to release. I would be different, I tell myself in my reverie, and therefore I would come different to this new place.

But only on rare cloudy days does yesterday's longing enter my space, slowing the rhythm of my dance, but not for long because I will not permit it to linger, not in that way. As knowledge and insight, however, it is always with me, an almanac for my now-life. This will bring rain, it tells me. That, sunshine. This will affirm. That, alienate. This will confuse. That, clarify. This advises pull back. That, hang on. This cautions, "Be still." That says, "Dance!"

We are always in the process of becoming, philosophers tell us, moving through one stage in preparation for the next. Each stage has its own purpose, our understanding of which ends delusional longing for previous stages. As with nature, so, too, with humankind. There are seasons in our lives we cannot bypass. We enter them when we are supposed to, and, once there, we do what we are supposed to do.

The first half century of my life was the "yes" season. I could not shape my lips to answer "no" to others' needs or remember how to say "yes" to my own. I was always interruptible, always accessible and available, always willing to stop working on a manuscript of my own and pull up, on my own computer no less, someone else's manuscript. I was like a plant from which one takes cuttings. A piece for this one. A piece for that one. A piece for those over there and these over here. Although there were times when I could feel the blade, I did not regret the cuttings. They strengthened my roots.

But there is a time when a plant should be left still, when the number of cuttings should be reduced, when it should be left undisturbed in the light of its own nourishing suns. That is the time now for me, and I am content in accepting that only now could the me-time have arrived. I believe I entered this season when I was supposed to. What remains is for me to do what I believe I am supposed to do: pick up the pen, or turn on the computer, and attempt to write.

When friends tell me that I should have tried to write years ago, planting seeds of regret in the earth of my feelings, I add rather than subtract, and the result is a full life of memories and experiences that form words and images I was not supposed to know, until now. Becoming older is a gift, not a curse, for it is that season when we have long and passionate conversations with the self we spoke to only briefly in our younger years. It could be argued that if gender politics changed, that is, if women in patriarchy weren't conditioned to be other-oriented, we could reach this season earlier in life. Perhaps that is true for some women, but not for me. Patriarchy did not force me to be maternal, and that is what I was, and am. Maternal. I chafe at the very idea that anyone would attribute this joy to patriarchy, to sexism, to restrictions on my life. If all the rules had been different, I know that my longer conversations would have been with my loved ones, my students, and others. That was my choice, and that was my joy. It was not so much that I held the joy of writing in suspension as that the season for writing had not yet arrived.

"I can't talk to you now," I say in this season. "I'm writing."

"This is not a good weekend for a visit," I am able now to tell friends. "I am driving up to the mountains to meditate and to write."

And to my own children, "Let me call you back later. I don't want to lose the words."

Those who love me are delighted rather than offended by the

new Gloria. They call and begin their conversation with, "I'm not going to talk long. I can hear in your voice you're busy." But they are certain enough of the availability of cuttings to feel comfortable saying, "I must talk to you now." "Hold on," I tell them. I leave the phone for the second it takes me to turn to my computer and save my document, and I return, the clock for the day turned face down in my heart.

Who or what I will become in this season is beyond my knowing, but I feel pregnant with the promise of new joys. I do not think they could equal the joys from my past, but they will be joys nonetheless, for as a woman thinketh, so is she in her heart. I think joy. I *choose* to think joy, and by so doing, I bring joy into my life.

I am calmer now. More introspective. More tolerant. More thoughtful. More observant. More expectant of success than fearful of failure. More aware of what I once called small details but which I now know are not small at all. I am different.

Here at midlife, I see in sharp, clear lines the primacy of every thought, every act, every person, every experience to my becoming and to my health. In my earlier life, I understood this intellectually. Now, I experience it spiritually.

I had always felt a sense of urgency about achievement, about getting things done, about finding all the answers, and bringing closure to all the conflicts, but here I measure achievement differently; it is less what someone says I should achieve and more what I want to achieve.

Here, I get things done, but in fuller appreciation of the process of doing them and the self that evolves therefrom.

Here, I search for answers, but with the understanding that each answer leads me to new questions. Indeed, having arrived here, I understand that living is the experience human beings have with questions. The nature of the questions we ask and the answers we offer are the statements we make about who we are in relation to ourselves, to others, and to the world in which we live. The questions end only when life ends — if either does.

Here, I have learned that closure is an act of the heart opening, not of the mind clarifying.

Here, I want no toxins in my heart or in my mind.

Here is the place for purging, for filtering, for distilling.

Here, I know that any diminishing of who I am will not result from the addition of years to my life, but rather from the senseless waste of self and talents, time and breath, that hatred, lack of forgiveness, selfishness, and materialism make of all lives, regardless of age. My heart has aged, but it has grown stronger. It loves with greater care, locking out no one and trying to beat with a fast and defensive pulse when it senses the approach of negative energy. It directs my hands to move in circles continuously in front of my face, protecting my spirit from harm. As smoke is used in African rituals to ward off evil spirits, so, too, do my hands circle.

Here, I have discovered the beauty of taking time to enjoy, with mindfulness, the Buddhists say, the ordinary joys of life, which are, in fact, our blessings.

Here, I feel a magical and inexplicable zest for life. Show me the mountain, and if it interested me, I would dare try to climb it.

As I sing a soon-sixty song, I hear the same chords of meaning I have sung all my singing life. They instruct me in how to work at living an examined life and how to *choose* joy. Because, of course, sadness has no rhythm to which wrinkled hands can clap and varicosed legs can dance, dance, dance!

Age

NIKKI GIOVANNI

we tend to fear old age
as some sort of disorder   that can be cured
with the proper brand of aspirin
or perhaps a bit of Ben-Gay for the shoulders
it does   of course   pay to advertise

one hates the idea of the first gray hair
a shortness of breath
devastating blows to the ego
indications we are doing
what comes naturally

it's almost laughable
that we detest aging
when we first become aware
we want it
little girls of four or five push
with eyes shining brightly at gram or mommy
the lie that they are seven or eight
little girls at ten worry
that a friend has gotten her monthly
and she has not
little girls of twelve
can be socially crushed
by lack of nobs on their chests
little boys of fourteen want
to think they want
a woman

the little penis that simply won't erect
is shattering to their idea of manhood
if perhaps they get a little peach fuzz
on their faces they may survive
adolescence proving there may indeed be life
after high school
the children begin to play   older
without knowing the price is   weariness

age teaches us that our virtues
are neither virtuous nor our vices
foul
age doesn't matter   really
what frightens is mortality
it dawns upon us that we can die
at some point it occurs we surely shall

it is not death we fear
but the loss of youth
not the youth of our teens
where most of the thinking took place
somewhere between the navel and the knee
but the youth of our thirties where career
decisions were going well
and we were respected for our abilities
or the youth of our forties
where our decisions proved if not right
then not wrong either
and the house   after all   is half paid

it may simply be that work
is so indelibly tied

to age that the loss
of work brings the depression
of impending death
there are so many   too many
who have never worked
and therefore for whom death
is a constant companion
as lack of marriage
lowers divorce rates
lack of life
prevents death
the unwillingness to try
is worse than any failure

in youth our ignorance gives us courage
with age our courage gives us hope
with hope we learn that man is more
than the sum of what he does
we also are what we wish we did
and age teaches us
that even that doesn't matter

The Affirmation

PATRICIA RAYBON

"Let's be pretty tonight."

A friend is on the phone, and we are planning for a party. We are going with our husbands to a fancy-dress dance, and we are dreaming about the evening.

"Let's be pretty tonight," she says, and her proposal releases a torrent of womanish chatter—talk of glittery earrings and sheer stockings, bare skin and lace, and perfume.

She will wear black velvet toreador pants with a black lace-mesh halter, a matador jacket, and high-heel shoes. I will wear high heels, too, and a long black velvet sheath with white lace sleeves and a beaded bodice cut low and off the shoulders.

My dress is two years old. But I've never worn it since I bought it, so it feels new. I feel new when I put it on, after a cool shower and a long rubdown with a clean, fresh towel. Then I pull the dress over my head and the silk lining slides over my skin like spring water.

This is a lovely gown and my breasts swell out of it—a brown woman's abundance; in the past, something to hide, to camouflage, to bind down tight. But when I walk down the stairs to the living room, my husband grabs me by the waist and kisses me on the lips, on my face, in my hair. You'll mess up everything, I tell him.

No, I won't, he says, then kisses me again. We are laughing.

At the hotel, inside the ballroom, I find my friend and, she, too, is laughing tonight and so is her husband. He likes his wife in the toreador pants and the lace mesh and the high heels, and he is teasing her, too, and pulling her toward him, embracing her and smelling her hair, her perfume.

We like this festiveness, and we are feeling something good, all of us—but my friend and I especially are bright and happy. We are feeling what it's like to love ourselves—two brown women, far past forty, born to an era that said we were all wrong.

Tonight we are "all" right.

Everything about us—not just our party clothes and our hair and our bright lipstick, not just all of that, but our understanding is right, too. We can be pretty tonight, and we can know it. It takes a long time for a brown woman to know that, or maybe even other women—other *people*—as well. It takes hard work and self-permission and self-love.

I am liking it a lot—this feeling, of not making excuses or worrying that something bad is reeking from my presence.

I am a good person, a loving wife, a strong mother, a good friend, a kind daughter, a loyal sister. And some days, life should be a fantasy. I can decide that right now, even for tonight.

So for tonight:

I am put together with stardust and good blood and fine genes, with the continuous urgings and tender pushes from ancestors and old friends and even the newly departed—loved ones, everyone.

I have a strong body, carved out of ebony and Jurassic amber, bronze and hard iron. My eyes are cut from diamonds. My hair is woven from the cattails of the Blue Nile, the hair under my arms and on my legs and between my legs is leaves of the konker tree and my eyelashes are the feathers of the great heron and my blood is the juice of the pomegranates and my muscles are the haunches of the leopard and my joints are the knees of mountain goats and the elbows of elephants and my feet are onyx, planted solid on a rock, or sometimes eagle's wings, lifting me up, up, up to soar and dip and fly.

I smell like the Earth and like the sweat of a fertile bride waiting for her virile groom and like all the flowers that ever bloomed and ever will bloom again and again. My heart is generous, so filled with forgiveness and hope that I can sing to children and shelter old women and hold old men in my arms and wipe away the regrets of their tears.

I can swim the Mediterranean Sea and scale McKinley and Piz Badile and Kilimanjaro and Aconcagua, and I ride St. Mary's glacier from her icy heights, across blue valleys as wide as rivers, and dip gracefully into the mouths of green lakes and call the trout and the rock bass and the walleye, and hear their words when they answer.

I am blessed by Jesus and I know the stories of Buddha and Brahma, the creator god, and Vishnu, the sleeping god, whose dream is the universe, and Horus and Isis and Osiris, and Gilgamesh, and Shiri ya Mwari, the Bird of God, and Shirichena, the Bird of Bright Plumage, and Mirthra, the god of light, and Orpheus, called "the Fisher" who fishes men, and Mumbo, the serpent god, and Shiva, who dances the holy dance. And I behold the Cross and ponder the Holy Grail and the Net of Indra, and I sit in the center of the Wheel of Fortune, anchored so firmly. And, like the Navajo, otherwise called the Dineh, I am on the pollen path. The heavenly pollen path.

Beauty above me, beauty below me, beauty to the left of me, beauty to the right of me. I am, like the Navajo, on the pollen path.

And I am pretty tonight.

No one in this room tonight is an enemy. They are all allies because I command it. They are all comrades because I believe it. They are all compatriots because we are all fighting for justice, goodness, and truth, and I mandate our mutual respect and understanding. If their deeds cause harm to anyone, I approach the offenders with love. If they won't hear my protest, I will melt their hearts with persistent love, with undying faith in their potential to be righteous and holy and good.

I know these things because I have the knowledge of the ages at my right hand and the wisdom of the universe at my left hand. And peace flows in me like a deep, blue river that I mount like a stallion and ride and ride into everlasting.

Now some will laugh at these things. They doubt such capacity, question such serenity, distrust such authority. But tonight when I take to the dance floor, can I help it if the parquet under my feet turns to gold and my onyx feet in a flash are transformed to eagle's wings and I then fly around the dance space, spinning and soaring and turning, moving to music composed just for me? It was written before I was born and I recognize it instantly, even before the first note is struck. It's my music, but I am filled with generosity, so I want to share it, to dance it with the others who've been waiting to move, longing to shake and jump and turn and roll.

So, I pull a woman with yellow hair from her seat and she grabs her husband, a man with black eyes, and he grabs a man with a kinky red beard and that man grabs his friend, an old woman with flowered skirts and seven teeth and a smile wide with knowledge and wisdom, who grabs a child who grabs her mother who grabs *her* mother who grabs an uncle who grabs his wife of forty years who reaches out both her hands to a line of people too long to count. All of them step onto the dance floor with me, all of them dipping and turning and rolling, and we are a great happy party — dancing and feeling our bodies and letting the sweat pour off of our bodies. Our glistening sweat, shining like diamonds in the night.

We are dancing, yes we are.

Dancing like the Ladakhi and the Apache and the Dineh.

Dancing like the Watusi and the Ogoni and the Ibo.

Dancing for all the years we didn't dance, certainly not together. Dancing to reclaim all the lost chances, all the harsh words, all the bad juju that ever passed between us. Dancing the future and its hopes into being.

I wave to my friend and she lifts her hands, acknowledging the truth of what I am seeing—nodding her head, yes! you are right. These things are true.

I hear her laughter across the room, and I catch it in my mouth and swallow it and the warmth of it is like a ballast that sets me right, lifting me even higher, making me twirl and whoop and sparkle in this beautiful, beautiful night.

From the heights, I watch myself dance, marveling at my grace and at my strong arms and lovely neck and my clear eyes and my remarkable strength.

I am stronger than a Sepik crocodile, more cunning than Gideon's three hundred, more powerful than David's five stones, brighter than the thunderbolts of Zeus.

I can change lives, resolve injustice, reverse poverty, inspire hearts and minds, connect kindred souls. I can make laughter and inspire singing, persuade lovers to find each other, strangers to make friends, and enemies to make peace. I can move mountains.

And God has given me permission to say these things and to write these things.

I will thus now, emboldened with the spirit of the ages, preach the good news to the poor, heal the brokenhearted, teach deliverance to the captives, recover sight to the blind, and set at liberty those that are bruised and defeated.

I can even tame a lion, snare it and pin it on its back and hold it down, until its bravado is quieted, its heavy breathing not even a whisper, its roar only soft moaning—more quiet than a hummingbird waiting to fly, softer than dew.

Every morning I wash the sky and sing the clouds aloft. Then I drink in the sunshine and I glow. So, it makes perfect sense, perfect logic.

I am pretty tonight. And these are the words, borrowed from

that man Joseph Campbell, a white man, the myth man—who borrowed it, in turn, from his dark heroes and dreamers, his seers and shamans, his priests and perceivers and potentates, then passed it on to believers such as me to describe this special night.

"Oh . . . ah . . ."

Journal (February 12, 1987)

ALICE WALKER

Another rainy night. I am in bed, where I've been for several hours, after a long walk through Ubud to the monkey forest and then for lunch at the Lotus Cafe—entirely inhabited by Europeans and Americans and one stray very dark and pretty Indian girl in a vivid red dress. Then the walk home, stopping in a local shop—where the woman proprietor is sweet and sells wonderful flowing cool and colorful pants. (Rebecca, on seeing them hanging near the street, immediately exclaimed, "Miss Celie's pants!") Anyway, the pants I liked, knee length, with the flowing grace of a sarong, she no longer had, but she urged me to try a kind of flowered jumpsuit, very long—before she showed me how to adjust it to my shape—and Western-influenced Balinese. It looked great, so I bought it.

But the rain threatens to get me down. In the mornings there is a little sun—nothing direct; in the afternoons there are quite heavy showers, which, even if they are warm and we can walk right through them, I find a little overwhelming after the third or fourth day. Also feeling down because I've drunk so much beer, since the water is considered unsafe except here at the house. And, Robert says, this is the week before my period!

Anyway, *very* out of sorts, for me. It's true I overheard the house-keeper (who travels everywhere with an umbrella against rain and sun) tell Rebecca she "don't like black," as Rebecca was saying how much she wants to "brown"; and I resent always being perceived as just another "rich" American tourist and importuned to buy at every turn when we are walking and even here at the house. But Ubud is beautiful! I've never seen anything like it. The green rice paddies, the soft bluish-gray skies, the people who've created the landscape, and themselves, graceful, friendly, amazingly mellow.

So much so it is a shock to realize that as recently as 1965 more than 100,000 of them killed each other after an attempted Communist coup in Jakarta.

Bali makes me think of Uganda. The same gentle countryside and gentle people; the same massacres and bloodbaths.

Robert wondered aloud why you don't see middle-aged people, only the young and the old. A lot of them would have been among the 100,000.

I have many bites! The ones on my feet are especially maddening. In my gloomier moments this morning I thought: If it's going to rain all the time and I have to suffer mosquitoes as well, I might as well be in Mendocino. (Not knowing that Northern California was experiencing the worst flooding in thirty years!) I felt very homesick, which Rebecca found astonishing. She has taken to Bali—the people, the landscape, the food—like the trouper she is. She is one of those old, old transparent souls the Universe radiates through without impediment, and so, wherever we go, within a week everyone seems aware of her presence. She walks in the rain as if it is sun.

Have been reading *Dancing in the Light*, by Shirley MacLaine; much of it is true, as I have experienced life, and a lot is straight Edgar Cayce. But it is sad to see her spirituality limited by her racialism. Indians and Africans have a hard time; especially Africans who, in one of her incarnations, frustrate her because they're not as advanced as she is! It is amusing to contemplate what the Africans must have thought of her.

But I don't care about any of this. In the kitchen, Ketut is making dinner, chicken satay. Rebecca and Robert are at a fire dance, to which I declined to go—pleading aching joints, footwear erosion, and mildew of the brain. The rain is coming down in torrents. Lightning is flashing. The house we've rented is spectacular: it faces a terraced hillside of rice paddies, two waterfalls, and coconut trees and is built in Balinese style but is huge by Balinese standards, I think. Two large bedrooms downstairs and an open-air one upstairs, with another great wooden hand-carved antique Balinese bed at one end. The roof is thickly thatched.

Two days ago I celebrated my forty-second birthday here, with the two people I love most in the world; we talked about my visit, before we left home, to a very beautiful Indian woman guru, who spoke of the condition of "judness." A time of spiritual inertia, of feeling thick, heavy, devoid of light. Yet a good time, too, because, well, judness, too, is a part of life; and it is life itself that is good and holy. Not just the "dancing" times. Nor even the light.

Thinking of this, hoping my loved ones are dry, and smelling dinner, I look up straight into the eye of a giant red hibiscus flower Ketut just placed—with a pat on my head—by the bed. It says: Just *be*, Alice. Being is sufficient. Being is All. The cheerful, sunny self you are missing will return, as it always does, but only *being* will bring it back.

Unlocking Midlife

JACKIE WARREN-MOORE

I'm collecting locks—deadbolts and hook eyes
Aching for the click click
Satisfied fit of the tumbler when the pieces fall into place
The puzzle piece
Gently—not jammed
Fits
And I see the picture for the first time
Understanding the skeleton key
That fits every door even
If it's not locked
Thrown open—the empty room beckons and I
Spread my big body all around it
I lounge and get comfortable
Sprawl out and dream
Of other doors
Yet unopened.

Games

JACKIE WARREN-MOORE

Nobody ever told me how fast the game was played—how it could
    end
on the pump pump pump of a heartbeat
Nobody ever said that the days
months years shot by like comets
and become fixed
in a night sky constellation you can only gaze at

Everybody neglected to say what each card meant
how it got dealt
the consequences of folding way too soon
Nobody put up signs
nothing popped up
on all the right roads
suddenly turned treacherous

nobody ever told me
lessons flew by
and I didn't take notes

bogarted my way into the game
bluffed my stuff
parlayed my hand
into a trump
I survived
weaving and dodging
running blindly
steadily moving from

one card to the next
house full of cards
prayed would never come tumbling
down upon
my unbowed head

nobody ever told me
you leave the game
with what you brought
held tight in your fist,
in your heart
butt naked and palm open
nothing sticks
everything falls away
nobody ever told me love was the
only right answer
to questions
I didn't even know to ask

nobody ever told me
how it could all begin
on the pump pump pump
of a heartbeat
each beat
a new hand
another chance
to begin
to love
to play the game.

What I Learned on the Way to Getting Old: Don't Tell Your Age and Other Lessons

ELYSE SINGLETON

A lifelong friend, who can be called anything but vain, stopped freely giving out her age at twenty-one. "People make assumptions," she said. "They have stereotypes."

Though I understood that assertion, I didn't embrace it. Also, when I was young my age was cool; it was the equivalent of the latest fashion.

Fifteen was *super* cool. I had finally gotten over puberty and knew if I couldn't be eight, fifteen was the next best thing. I was young, gifted, and black. My future was going to be great because America had outlawed racism and soon being African American would be no less acceptable than being Jewish. I had endless potential, everything to look forward to, and only two problems. But then everybody has parents.

Sixteen was okay, too. I graduated from high school a year early. I couldn't wait to go off to college and get away from those two problems.

I told my age then to anyone who asked. I told anything to anyone who asked. There wasn't much to tell, and I was flattered by any interest.

By eighteen, I thought I should be doing more. I had heard of people writing novels at eighteen. I was going to school, absorbing but not producing.

Nineteen made me nervous. What did I have to gain? Being eighteen had made me an adult and able to vote (for a Democrat, of course). I liked that. In some states, I could legally smoke, drink, and have sex. And I could also make generous use of one of the first words I ever learned: "no." So, why did I need another year? What the heck was I supposed to do with nineteen? And I still had not done anything impressive that would compensate for the added chronological mileage. It would have been all right if people could say, "Look at her, at nineteen she's the youngest person ever to win the Pulitzer right after collecting her Ph.D. in astrophysics from Harvard!"

When I turned twenty, my college friends gave me a party to cheer me up. It didn't work. Then I understood in a real and visceral way that my birth year would remain the same as each coming year marched away from it.

I learned too late that ageism is the dumbest prejudice anyone can ever have. Unless you die very young, it turns on you. It would have been smarter to be bigoted against Puerto Ricans or Asians or gays because I will probably not grow into a Puerto Rican or Asian or gay. But, of course, barring early expiration, I will grow old.

As a kid, I didn't know I was being influenced by biases that go back to an evolutionary period in which youth equaled strength to survive and survival was all that mattered. Life was short and brutish instead of longer and brutish the way it is today. People were considered old at forty because most were dead by forty.

For the first part of my life, as long as my age had a one or two in front of the second digit, I would gladly tell it. Now that has changed. I am not as casual even though it goes against the grain of the times.

In an "open" era in which people seem to have opened up their heads and let their brains spill out, revealing their most personal secrets, age is just a minor statistic to be rattled off. Or is it? Decades ago, women routinely hid their ages. I remember when as a little kid I excitedly blurted out, in a bakery shop, that it was my mother's twenty-sixth birthday. She was a bit unnerved.

Today that seems silly. But really, what has changed since then? Is this now a world in which age doesn't matter and in which it is no more difficult to be black than to be Jewish? Are people more evolved? Or is it a planet on which not a day goes by that the evening news does not broadcast fresh examples of the gross cruelty human beings perpetrate against one another?

I have learned that it is a world in which women should be read their Miranda rights before revealing their ages. Because what we say can and will be held against us. I have heard women say that after forty, they feel discounted.

They see the looks of dismissal or the knowing glances that mean a person feels he or she now understands something really far-reaching about you because you've fielded a simple number. When you are over thirty-five, some feel as if they've got something on you, that they know your Achilles' heel.

My mother said she lied about her age after forty because she was tired of hearing, "You don't look that old." It's the common backhanded compliment for people who look youthful, as black people often do. And, unfortunately, hearing it makes a person feel that old.

But men are granted an amnesty from aging. Hollywood—both cultural mirror and dictator of American values—has helped make this inequity a social gold standard.

Mainstream movies never cast a leading lady over fifty, and seldom over forty, to play a romantic role, though leading men can be seventy. Twenty and thirty years sometimes separate love interests. In a mid-1990s remake of *Camelot*, the young Julia Ormond was cast in the classic with Richard Gere and Sean Connery. So, Lady Guinevere's suitor was old enough to be her father and her fiancé was old enough to be her grandfather. She goes to a nunnery at the end—good choice.

One year *Playboy* made a big to-do of featuring a centerfold who was over forty. Yes, that's quite generous of them, considering that Hugh Hefner, the fellow who runs the operation, could be a forty-year-old's grandpa and, when he appears in his trademark lounging jacket, now looks like some poor fellow who has wandered away from a nursing home.

Nevertheless, the age-gender double standard remains a pop culture mandate. And pop culture shapes and dictates the attitudes of most Americans. That's why they call it popular. When you are an unpopular age, it is best to beware.

In my first novel, *This Side of the Sky*, a character coming of age during World War II fails to disclose something about herself to get a job she never would have gotten otherwise. She's light-skinned and passes for white. I wrote about the situation sympathetically, though it is one completely alien to me. I or any member of my family could sooner pass as an ink spot than a white person. Yet, I understand what it means to want to be who you are and still be treated fairly.

If life is a game, one goal is to avoid penalties, especially for things you cannot help. It's not that my friends won't always know how old I am or about other acts I wouldn't share with acquaintances or strangers. But I am far beyond the naïveté that would make me think that when I am out in the world at large I am among friends.

Instead of expending energy reacting to other people's reactions, I want the time and mental space to cultivate a comfort with myself that is unshakable, regardless of age. Of course, that brings up the question of how I will accept my age while declining to reveal it to others. I admit that will take a few emotional and philosophical contortions. However, being black and female in America requires grappling with a lot of paradoxes. What's one more?

I have learned that the future is not the postal carrier of social change but the challenger of past hopes and dreams. So, what am I going to do with those "extra" years past forty as I sail into the wild blue yonder of aging? I am not going to wrestle with society about its ignorant prejudices. I will be too busy making those hopes and dreams come true.

Midlife Blues

CARMEN TURNER

When I turned fifty years old, I accepted it with trepidation and sorrow. Standing at midlife and looking back on my journey to this point, I realize that the aspirations and dreams I had for myself have not yet come to fruition. The melancholy I feel is indescribable. I have had more than my share of hardship and pain. The mainstay of the pain is the lifelong depression I have suffered. Years of depression that slowly eroded my self-esteem, vitality, and ambition. My melancholia results from a combination of a chemical imbalance in the brain and childhood abuse. I am a survivor of physical, emotional, and sexual abuse.

I first became aware of being depressed when I was about ten or eleven years old. I remember sitting on my bed, crying and rocking myself, wishing I were dead. I was the victim of my mother's moods and rage. Living with her was like constantly walking on eggshells. One never knew what kind of mood she would be in or what could set her off. She seemed to hate me, and I was often an object of that hate. I wasn't a bad child, but it seemed that I could never do anything right for her. She often threatened to put me in a home for delinquent girls. I knew she got this idea from a friend of hers who had put her daughter in such a home. When she wasn't threatening me, she was physically abusing me. Her constant threats of abandonment and her violence led me to believe that I was not worthy of her or anyone else's love.

I believe that my depression kicked in with a vengeance when I gave up my dream to dance professionally because of severe stage fright and anxiety attacks. I had thrown away my talents and dreams. Nevertheless, I was always able to get good jobs—claims examiner, assistant buyer, and medical assistant were just a few. I later started doing temporary work—as a receptionist and secretary. Later, as a professional union waitress, I made decent money, but it was mindless and uncreative work. The daily cash tips I made seemed to match the transient lifestyle I had acquired. I would quit one job and find another one the next day.

Even though I worked every day, I was often behind in rent and bills. I ran from job to job, apartment to apartment, and man to man. I knew I was unhappy, but I didn't know why. I was tired of being tired and blue. There were days when I couldn't get out of bed. On the days I did try to go to work, nothing looked right on my size seven figure. I hid my unhappiness and low self-esteem with fabulous clothes and expensive makeup. God forbid if people found out that I didn't have myself together.

I dated men I knew wouldn't want a serious relationship: drug dealers, players, and men who would not commit. I was square as a pool table and just as green, and I found this type of man fascinating. I feared intimacy and yet I was promiscuous. I longed to be loved, but I would run from the stable, kind, and good men for fear of being abused, used, or abandoned.

In the early eighties, my condition had deteriorated to the point that I often thought about suicide. I didn't want to live anymore. I was tired of the merry-go-round I was on, but I couldn't seem to get off. I was angry with God for all the pain and suffering I felt. I didn't understand why he insisted that I continue to live. I felt like Job lamenting my predicament and questioning God's wisdom.

I first sought help during this time. My early therapists were good, but if you're not willing to do the work, you won't get well. I had to really dig inside myself on the issues that caused me so much pain. I had stuffed so much crap down inside of me that I couldn't talk about those things. I was angry because I had stopped dancing; angry because of the abuse I had suffered; and angry with myself for allowing it to happen. My mother's prediction that I was no good and would never amount to anything had come true, and the pain of that reality was eating away at my very soul. My therapist offered me medication, but I turned it down, feeling I could handle things without it.

It wasn't until 1992 that I decided to go on medication. Well, I didn't decide. I had no choice. I was constantly plagued with black, ominous thoughts of death and I could not stop crying. One day I woke up with tears running down my face. I showered, dressed, and rode the bus to work with silent tears. A very dear friend of mine saw me and suggested I immediately get on some kind of medication to pull me out of this hell I was in. It was the best advice I ever got.

Prozac was all the rage at the time. Skeptical, I took it. Depression is insidious in that if you don't do something about it, it just gets worse. Before I started my medication, my inner dialogue with myself was always negative, "Oh, I'm so stupid, I can't do anything right, why should I try—things always go wrong for me." I had gone through so much that I couldn't fathom myself living the life I wanted to live. There was a hopelessness I felt that is beyond explaining. When the Prozac kicked in, it was like the sun rays burning away the black, negative clouds from my brain, allowing the light in. I could finally think clearly and rationally. Life no longer seemed hopeless.

I have now been in therapy off and on since the mid-eighties. And it hasn't been easy. It's work looking for the right therapist. You want someone you can trust and feel comfortable with. I have had white therapists and black therapists. My first therapist was a young white woman. She worked in a clinic that was run by a black woman. It would take me half an hour to warm up to her and then my time would be up. I stopped going to her when she was insensitive about an incident that was very painful for me. She apologized and begged me to come back, but I refused. My second therapist was a black woman, Dr. Romaria Tidwell, whom I had requested from a service that places clients with professionals. I immediately felt at ease with her and trusted her. Unfortunately, my finances didn't allow me to continue seeing her.

It has been my experience that when I requested a black professional, I was often disappointed. One sister, whom I liked, refused to see me after I lost a job. Another turned out to be very unprofessional, which was a major disappointment since I had left a white therapist, thinking that I needed to be with a therapist who understood the black experience and the special issues that black women face.

Ultimately, what matters is not the color of the professional, but how she or he interacts with you, how you relate to her or him, and whether you feel that person can help you. But, for a black woman going into therapy for the first time who may have reservations about the whole process, I would suggest she find a person of color.

I now know what triggers my depression and the things I need to do to keep that from happening. One of those triggers is financial instability. A good part of my depression had been brought on by lack of funds and my hand-to-mouth weekly existence that went on for years. Constantly worrying about how I was going to pay my rent and bills took a toll on me—mentally, psychologically, emotionally, and physically. I have taken the necessary steps so I can be more in control of the financial part of my life. I have upgraded my job skills and am now a legal assistant. This allows me to command a bigger salary and have more stability. I'm finally learning to set money aside and I'm boning up on the world of investing.

Another trigger for depression was my weight. Because of my condition and lack of money, I often found myself sitting at home in front of the TV, constantly eating. I managed to eat myself into a size eighteen dress. Embarrassed about my appearance, I avoided social gatherings where I could possibly meet people and make friends. If I did do anything, it was often alone—I went to museums or the movies. I would occasionally go out with a female friend to dinner or an art opening. I knew I had to get my eating under control and stop isolating myself because of it.

I'm now eating better, exercising, and buying clothes that I feel good in. I'm getting out more and enjoying myself. I'm more accepting and loving of myself, and I know with this acceptance the weight will come off.

I am now on maintenance—meaning that I'm just on medication. I go once a month to see a psychiatrist who writes my prescription, and we talk briefly about how I feel and how I'm doing on the medication. According to my doctor, I may have to be on medication for the rest of my life, and that's all right with me. But I'm no longer in therapy. I decided to take a break from it and utilize the natural solutions that are available to me. I have started yoga, and I'm using homeopathic remedies and aromatherapy to help regulate my moods and weight. I'm establishing a closer relationship with God—through reading, prayer, and fellowship.

My depression ebbs and flows like the tide. I know what triggers that tide and I know what to do about its ebb. I am now fifty-one years old. I'm more gentle, loving, and forgiving of myself and others. My short, chic hairstyle is now streaked with silver. My nickname is still Beautiful, although some days I ain't feeling it. I'm learning to not define myself by how others view me or treat me. I'm no longer giving away my power. I'm learning how to nurture myself—something I never received growing up.

Acknowledging such things as these in midlife is bittersweet. I rejoice in the fact that I have survived the worst of times, and I'm looking forward to the second half of my life and all its possibilities with hope, peace, and wisdom.

How to Fly into Fifty
(Without a Fear of Flying)

S. PEARL SHARP

Change something: cut your hair, put different art on your walls.

Go dancing to '50s or '60s music, and remember when.

Get Touched! Spend an afternoon at the spa, get a massage, pedicure, manicure, facial.

Make a list of all the obstacles you've survived in fifty years.

List your accomplishments—things that show you've been here on the planet.

Read a poem to someone, have someone read a poem to you.

Dine with Nature—go on a picnic.

Call a friend (who is older than you) just to say "Hi."

Spend an afternoon with someone younger than twelve.

Contemplate how your life has changed in the last twenty years, then get rid of everything you no longer need.

Get a complete physical checkup.

Kiss someone at the exact moment that marks your birth.

Buy fresh flowers for your nest.

Enjoy an old-fashioned chocolate malt or root beer float.

Buy an article of clothing that is sassier than the regular you. Wear it with an attitude!

Hug someone every day for fifty days.

Hug yourself twice a day for fifty days.

Plan ahead: create an astounding wish for your birthday cake candle blowout.

Develop a welcome ritual for new gray hairs.

Learn a current love song.

Make love.

Buy yourself a present.

Set aside time to meditate: think on the glory of fifty.

Do something each month of this year to celebrate turning fifty. Try to do it on the same day as your birth date.

Select a PMA (positive mental attitude) that will help you through the next 364 days. Write it down, paste it on the bathroom mirror or refrigerator, then say it out loud every day.

The Ball of a Lifetime

TRUDIER HARRIS-LOPEZ

When I was approaching "the Big 5-0," I decided that I wanted to do something unusual to celebrate. A friend had turned sixty the year before and had given herself a huge dinner party with jazz band playing. I decided that that was the motif I wanted to pursue. So, I started the process of organizing a fiftieth birthday ball—*ball*, not party. There were so many balls that I had missed as a teenager and young adult because I was the classic nerd, always more interested in studying than dancing. It was finally time, I thought, for the tide to turn.

Many people were surprised that I was so gleeful about celebrating my fiftieth birthday. I credit that to my mother, who always insisted that one tell the truth about one's age and be thankful that God had allowed you to live as long as you had (that means even more these days with so many of my friends and colleagues having died in the past couple of years). So, I determined that the occasion warranted class, which would be manifested in a memorable space, with memorable company, and even more memorable music. Now, in small-town Chapel Hill, North Carolina, one's options are limited in such a desire for classiness. Still, I wanted to celebrate in the town where I had lived and worked for over two decades.

The hotel I selected, the Siena, is a small luxury hotel with a ballroom that would hold perhaps two hundred people comfortably. That was fine. My final guest list reached about one hundred fifty. With its Italian influence—the hotel is modeled after a sister facility in Italy—the large-patterned comfort of the rugs and furniture meshed well with the overall atmosphere I wanted to create. And what special luck that the hotel actually had February 27, 1998, free. Even more perfect, that day was a Friday. Party time!

With the hotel selected, I went dress shopping. Now, you can't just wear any old dress-up dress to your fiftieth birthday ball, so this search was serious. It was especially serious for me because I am *not* a shopper. Shopping for me is a grudging necessity. I go only when I need something. And that was the case in this instance. The difference was that the need was defined by desire, so I actually experienced what some of my shopping friends must go through every time they set foot in a mall. After searching all over creation, I ended up in a shop in Durham, North Carolina, appropriately named "Images," where I found the perfect gown. It was Zeta Blue, floor length, with spaghetti straps, and a form-fitting sequined blue top that flowed out from the waistline into yards of material ample enough to accommodate my generous African hips. The added touch was a sheer, long-sleeved, floor-length matching jacket/coverlet that the wearer could use or take off for dramatic effect. When the friend who was helping me plan the ball put her seal of approval on the gown, I gave up about half a month's salary and purchased it.

With that settled, the serious detail work began—guest list, food selection, invitations, decorations, music, guest book, hostesses, and, best of all, the birthday cake. The guest list was easy. I invited friends, family, and colleagues from all over the Southeast. It was such a pleasure to realize that only a few of the nearly one hundred sixty folks who had been invited were unable to come. Several family members came from Alabama, and friends came from Georgia, particularly Atlanta, Washington, D.C., Richmond and Harrisonburg, Virginia, and from all over the state of North Carolina. A friend from Jackson, Mississippi, was on her way by car when a thunderstorm in Birmingham, Alabama, forced her to give up and return home; she composed a special poem for the occasion and had it framed and sent to me. I received greetings from across the United States and from as far away as Nigeria.

With so many favorable responses to the invitation, I knew I had to have absolutely wonderful food. My planning buddy and I selected roast beef (literally, a fourth of a cow), jumbo shrimp, smoked salmon, crab cakes, chicken, asparagus, endive with cheese, and cheese and fruit trays. Some of my fondest memories are of the beautiful displays of food, the special carving station for roast beef, and the cake-cutting station. A friend from the D.C. area made herself famous at the ball for her love of the crab cakes and another made herself equally well known for her love of the smoked salmon.

Just outside the ballroom, at one end of the hotel's rather expansive lobby, we set up the bar. That choice carries a story in itself. When friends of a friend learned that I was going to have an "open bar" at my birthday ball, they wanted her to convey to me that they thought I was crazy. "People will drink her into the poor house," they asserted. Well, I insisted on the open bar, and it was the right decision. Since it was outside the ballroom, and since I was not about to set up any kind of monitoring system, it meant that hotel guests who were inclined to do so decided to join our ball. So what if we spent a few drinks that way? Everybody had a good time. And the bar area allowed us to meet some folks we would not otherwise have encountered. Dick Vitale was in town to call the Carolina–Duke basketball game, and he dropped by for a brief chat because he knew the leader of the band I had hired for the occasion. (In the elevator on the way down to the ballroom, I met another celebrity—Ted Koppel and his college-age daughter.) The band called itself "Liquid Pleasure," and the music was just as smooth as the name implies. Masters of 1960s tunes and just about everything else you can imagine, they were at that time one of the five most requested bands in the United States for sorority and fraternity functions. The leader of the band is the son of a friend who was once my nurse and who is still the musician at my former church. They had folks up and shaking their booties until way after midnight. The bandleader is famous for his imitations of Louis Armstrong and Elvis Presley, so the group was a hit all around. Of the many special memories I have of the musical encounters that evening, one is of me sitting in for the drummer, pretending to be talented. Another is being serenaded by the daughter of my planning buddy. Yet another is of being serenaded by a church member whom I had no idea could sing. And of course there was the moment during which a special song was played, and my friend and I were allowed to have the dance floor to ourselves.

Now, of course, if one plans a ball, one must have an escort suitable to the occasion. Since I was not actively dating at the time, the brother of a friend of mine consented to be my escort. He was resplendent in his tuxedo and was the perfect gentleman for the occasion. We arrived early, greeted folks as they arrived, and partied heartily. He was a nice man, but there wasn't any chemistry there beyond the evening.

I had reserved several rooms at the hotel for guests. It was in my older sister's room that I dressed for the occasion. A niece focused on makeup (very little) while my younger sister succeeded in getting my locks up and pinned with the silver accessory that I had selected to accompany the gown. My older sister had brought me a wrist bouquet, and she took care of making sure that was in place. I had purchased long, dangling silver earrings and selected my "sexy shoes" for the occasion: three-inch spikes without backs. They are the kind of shoes you wear for show for a couple of hours, then get down and relax by changing into shoes with lower heels or into dancing socks; I did the latter (hey, it was my ball).

When guests arrived, they were greeted by the two young ladies I had selected to be junior hostesses. One of them was my grandniece and the other was the young lady I was mentoring at the time in the Chapel Hill–Carrboro School system. One was dressed in cream and the other in black; both were done up like little movie stars. They were in charge of the guest book in which ballgoers offered their best wishes. They were also in charge of directing people to where they could leave their gifts. (In spite of numerous directives to the contrary, folks insisted upon bringing gifts to the ball.)

If you're going to party at a ball, you have to party in a place with impressive decorations. I owe mine to Balloons and Tunes, to whom I gave responsibility for making the very air dance with excitement. They filled the place with purple, gold, and green balloons, hanging them from the ceiling as well as bunching them in clusters on the tables, and they extended the theme to the small patio off the ballroom (which we were able to use because it was seventy degrees that evening in February). Most fortunate of all, the day before they were scheduled to decorate, they received a new order of gold balloons that had "50" printed, in various typefaces, on each one of them. When they were blown up, it was indeed a sight to see. The image of balloons among beautifully dressed guests dancing with their partners is one that I will treasure.

Now, a birthday ball cannot be a birthday ball without an unforgettable birthday cake. And this cake was the cake to end all cakes. My planning buddy and I met with the owner of A Cake Tray, the cake service, and spent an afternoon sampling twelve of her special flavors. We even brought samples away to keep on testing until the selection was completed. Finally, we settled on white Frangelico hazelnut for the bottom cake and chocolate fudge decadence for the elevated top cake. The shape of the cake, however, was all me. I decided that I wanted a large square bottom cake, frosted in a gold crisscrossing pattern. The top cake was to be set at an angle and, in keeping with my life as a scholar and writer, made in the shape of an open book. It was to be frosted in white with gold trimming and be about two feet wide and eight inches high. On the left side of the top cake, I directed the baker to inscribe my name and the date, place, and time of my birth. On the right side, she inscribed the legend: "Turning 50 . . . a distinction with a difference" (with respect to Toni Morrison) and underneath that a famous quote from Zora Neale Hurston: "You got to go there to know there." In contrast to my expectation that there would be lots of cake left over, it was all gone about an hour after it was cut, and I never got to taste it. Thank goodness for the photographs!

In fact, photographs were the order of the evening. My official photographer was one of my sisters from Alabama. Another sister also took pictures, as did a niece. Friends, friends, and more friends also snapped shots, so that I have a host of photographic memories from that occasion. A really striking one is of "the Wintergreen Women," a group of twelve to fourteen African American women writers from Virginia and North Carolina. We gather in the mountains of Wintergreen, Virginia, every May for a time-out from the business of academia and other matters that occupy our lives. Seven of the Wintergreen Women came to the ball. Most striking of all was that, without consultation, we all wore gowns or dresses that echoed a blue/black theme.

All the out-of-town guests who were still around on Saturday morning were invited to my house for breakfast. The first of about twenty folks arrived shortly before 9 A.M. for sausage casserole, croissants, and fruit salad. By the time they had to leave at 9:30, others were arriving. Although the last person ate at midday, the celebrating went on until about 4 P.M., when friends from Atlanta finally drew themselves away from the conversation and headed for the highway.

Hosting a ball for myself, my family, my friends, and colleagues prepared me well to enter postfifty existence. I had encountered too many women who constantly hid their ages and who were fearful of moving toward greater maturity. I had no such qualms. Indeed, many of my acquaintances were shocked to learn that I was fifty. Now, I am fifty-four. I credit my ball, in part, for how I have spent the past four years of my life. I never dread getting older; I simply plan for it through retirement options. And I never lost sight of the possibility that, yes, indeed, one day I would join the ranks of married women. That occurred in 2001. In a whirlwind romance (I think that's the only way I could have done it), I met a man in Jamaica and married him six weeks later (I know, I know: Stella, Stella—but without the age gap). As of this writing, we are about to celebrate our first anniversary.

Of course, I would not be so disingenuous as to assert that my birthday ball was responsible for everything that's happened since then. I do assert, however, that any human being who has reached the ripe "old" age of fifty should celebrate in a special way. I constantly encourage anyone I meet to do so. (I'm working on my dentist right now.) If one arrives at fifty sane and healthy, then one has an obligation of sorts to mark that occasion (I felt the same way when I insisted that my older sister and her husband celebrate their fiftieth wedding anniversary a few years ago; they were planning to just let it go by). You will surely never pass that way again.

Some folks might think it a bit arrogant to host a ball for oneself. But I ask, "Who is going to come along and volunteer to do it for me?" I had spent twenty-five years before I turned fifty preparing lectures for college classes, grading papers and exams, writing letters of recommendation, publishing articles and books, serving on countless committees, consulting far and wide, attending numerous conferences, traveling all over creation, and generally neglecting my personal life in favor of my profession; surely I could pause for once and focus on *me*. I deserved it. I had a good time doing it. In spite of one friend's assertion that I should never host a ball again because there is no way I could top what I did in 1998, I still can't wait to turn sixty and give it a try.

In Search of Meaningful Work

JAN THOMAS

I started working for the telephone company right after college, when I was twenty-two. In the company's one-hundred-plus-year history, I was the first African American hired into a management position in the advertising department, and I got the job because, unlike some of my competitors, minority and white, I didn't vomit or pass out during the preliminary exam.

Looking back, I probably should have seen problems coming. The fact that retaining the contents of my stomach was a key factor in the hiring process should have given me a clue. But I was young, and I didn't know any better. At the time, I thought any job was a good job. Following that premise, a job that paid twenty-three thousand dollars per year had to be great.

Part of that mind-set came from watching too much television. I'd grown up in the sixties and early seventies, so my view of work was influenced as much by the media as it was by what I experienced at home. Even though I'd worked summer jobs since I was a teenager, I entered the workforce believing that working outside the home would either be the same never-ending slice of hell that my mother often described or a series of exciting, generally pleasant adventures like those befalling Pamela Ewing, Krystal Carrington, and the other soap opera divas I watched on TV. For those women, it seemed that the road to success was paved with hair spray.

I started at the phone company in the eighties when money was god, greed was good, and image was everything. You could have whatever you wanted as long as you were driven enough, thin enough, pretty enough—and sported a great hairdo. I was naïve enough to believe that. I knew nothing of middle ground.

During my first years on the job, I stuck to those convictions. I wore fancy pumps and tailored suits with stiff, pretty blouses and fluffy bow ties. At times, I worked from eight in the morning till two the next day. I accepted projects that didn't excite me; I followed a career path that someone else chose. I was a cog in the wheel, and I knew it, but on paydays, at least, life seemed pretty damn good.

By my thirties, though, the bloom was starting to fade on my corporate rose. Work-related friendships proved fragile. Job security ebbed and flowed. Coworkers drifted off to other places. Most went to other companies, and more than a few took the scenic route there: through divorce court, psychological counseling, and rehab. I stayed away from the serious stuff, but by the time I was thirty-five, my drink du jour was a swig of Mylanta with a stiff Advil chaser.

Without seeing it coming, I was turning into one of the angry little people I'd met and disdained during my first few years at the phone company. I was becoming the type of person who methodically counted down the days until retirement—even though, at the time, I had more than ten years to go. I finally understood my mother's frustration. Like her, I began to speak bitterly of losing my dreams. My anger didn't come from the fact that my job lacked value. It was public relations, admittedly, not brain surgery, but someone had to do it, and I did it quite well.

The problem stemmed from getting older. I ran headfirst into the fact that, no matter who we are or what we do or what choices we make, there comes a point when we all have to question our decisions. Things like "relationships" and "meaning" and "passion" were becoming increasingly important. Titles and possessions started to lose their appeal.

I chucked the power pumps for sensible shoes and a pocket Day-timer. I joined the herd that believed that marriage and having babies were the things to do. Single people like me got married; married people started families; and several women who used to despise children chose not to come back to work after giving birth.

Those who didn't have children began a search for meaning as well. One friend of mine walked away from the company after more than twenty years on the job. She said she wanted to find a job that allowed her to give something back to society. She sold her house, moved to Kansas City (she'd always wanted to live there), and eagerly took a job with a nonprofit company for less than half of her former salary. Another woman sold all of her possessions and joined the Peace Corps.

I, too, wanted to make a difference. I wanted to leave a legacy. I wanted to know I'd done something more with my life than help a handful of people get rich. Eventually, that need for meaning drove me out. Like my friend, I left the company after twenty years and joined a nonprofit. The salary isn't great, but the work is more rewarding and I have enough free time to pursue things that really matter. In my own way, I'm following my mother's path. She started a second career in her sixties and now spends most of her time helping children from the inner city. She doesn't get paid, but she says the satisfaction she receives is priceless.

When I worked at the phone company, I couldn't drive by the building on a Saturday or Sunday without losing my breath. Now, I zip by without gasping, but my eyes are drawn to the people who litter the entryway like roadkill.

Whenever I catch the gaze of one of the older folks, I hope to see a companionable gleam in their eyes. I hope that, like me, they've forged a truce—easy or not—with their choices.

When I look at the youngsters, though, I often feel a pang of pity as I watch them plod through the revolving doors, sporting attitude and wearing the corporate uniform du jour.

I wish I could tell them what a middle-aged mentor once told me: that my life wouldn't mirror those of the television celebrities I idolized. That, in the long run, only a handful of people succeed by keeping others down.

I wish I could tell these young corporate wanna-bes that, given the opportunity to live my life over again, I'd pursue meaningful work earlier. I'd appreciate, sooner, the value of giving back.

According to most reports, Americans work more than the citizens of any other industrialized country in the world. We have longer workdays, we work on weekends, and we take fewer and shorter vacations. We're hugely productive, and we have a right to be proud. There's nothing wrong with being a damn fine cog on a damn fine wheel—at least for a while.

But one day, if we live long enough, we're all going to have to look in the mirror and ask, "What have I done?" Those of us who fail to ask that question in our twenties and thirties must be prepared to pay up in middle age.

Of course, maybe that's not so bad. There's something liberating about looking at your life from the backside. It's easier to be decisive and to make hard choices. It's impossible to ignore the value of time.

During my career at the phone company, I spent more than 65,000 hours at work. I can't get any of those hours back, but I know enough, in middle age, to avoid making the same mistakes again.

And I know enough to pay attention, this time, when my elders tell me that I'll have to look in the mirror again one day. The question, they say, will be the same one. *What have I done?* But when I ask it, the odds of having the time to make other choices will be slim to none.

But they tell me not to worry. They pat my hand the same way I'd probably pat the hands of people twenty years younger than I.

You're still just a baby, the elders tell me.

You still have plenty of time.

Dreaming of Crones

CARLEEN BRICE

I've always had rich dreams full of fascinating and memorable images. Dreams bright enough to illuminate myself to myself. And I have always tried to pay attention to what they could teach me.

As a young woman, my dreams often reflected my fears of not measuring up to the expectations I had of myself, and the expectations I thought others had of me. I often had nightmares in which I just barely saved someone from harm. I also regularly dreamed I was in a house with hidden doors that allowed people to enter my home without my knowledge or consent, making me feel exposed and vulnerable.

By day, I thrived on anxiety. Seeking approval from my then-boyfriend, I hauled my butt to the gym five days a week and developed a firm, strong body. Seeking approval from bosses, I stressed deadlines and worked hard and did well in my career. Seeking approval from friends, I tried to be helpful and funny and established relationships with good people. Insecurity paid off for me.

But at night, my subconscious would let me know how overwhelmed I was by all the dos and don'ts I lived by. It's hard work to always do the "right" thing and look the "right" way. What if I let someone down? What if someone saw me as I really was? My God, what if I forgot to be perfect?

It's a common fear that little black girls and grown black women live with. Many of us were taught that to be accepted, we have to be as good as or better than white people. We have to be smarter and work harder than they do if we want to be treated merely as well. As women, we are led to believe our only assets are our youth and beauty. We must look good and be good. Always.

These racist, sexist, and deeply false assessments of our worth can make us buckle under the weight of the myth of the Black Superwoman or keep us locked into the stereotype of the un-educated, unwed, welfare mother, afraid to try, afraid to hope. I struggled for years to meet some unspoken standard of African American womanhood.

Then my mother died.

She had just turned forty-five (I was on the brink of thirty) and it stunned me when she died so young from breast cancer. Her death made me judge everything I did as perhaps the last thing I would do. I had quit my full-time job to take care of her and had no desire to get a new one. I couldn't see spending precious time shackled to a desk. I worked part-time jobs to give me time to write essays, poems, and short stories, most of which were pretty bad. But that didn't matter. What counted is that I was being true to myself. I also stopped obsessing about how I looked, refusing to waste energy on such an empty cause. I stopped walking miles to nowhere on the treadmill and went for long walks outside, sustaining my body and soul. I ate foods that were satisfying, as well as healthy, and allowed my body to settle at the weight it wanted.

For three years after my mother died, I struggled to get my then-boyfriend to understand and like the "new me." I wanted him to appreciate the woman who was no longer afraid of losing his ap-proval. I wanted him to be proud of the woman who was willing to risk failure and was daring enough to be flawed. But he never did. Toward the end of our relationship, we decided to buy a house. I suspect we thought a home would fix what was wrong between us, would bind us together with cement and brick. I kept falling in love with old, broken-down houses. I thought they had character. To ex-plain my preference for what surely were money pits, I told him,

"It's like someone who has a gap between her teeth. If you care for her, the gap only becomes part of her charm; it makes her more interesting." He didn't get it. "I could never love someone with a gap between her teeth," he replied.

Oh, honey, we all have gaps somewhere.

That's when I realized it wasn't my job to convince him; my responsibility was to act on what I knew. So, I bought myself a house with droopy gutters and a fence that leans to the south like it's trying to warm itself. And I met my husband. A man who believes the gods have blessed me with a round belly and full ass. A man who knows about gaps.

And my dreams started to change. Now, when I find a door in my dream, it leads me to hidden treasures, rooms full of furniture, clothes, china, silver, and other finery. A week after I got married at thirty-five, I dreamt I was at the theater. Ten wizened women appeared on stage, and I realized they were going to strip. At first, I was shocked and horrified. Then the women began to sway and turn and remove their old-lady dresses, slips, and stockings. And it was natural and wonderful. They stood before the crowd— shriveled, sagging bodies on display—with no fear and no shame. When they finished, one of the women, small and dark as a blackberry, took off her wig and showed the few wisps of white hair that still clung to her head. The audience applauded and rushed to the stage. I went to the tiny woman and bent down and kissed her almost-bald head and told her she was beautiful.

One night, as I was about to fall asleep, these words went through my head:

My hair is nappy.
My feet are dirty.
There is hair under my arms.
I am letting myself go.

And getting my self back. I'm living the lesson I started to learn after my mother died. I'm not all the way there, of course. Those dancing crones know things that I can't possibly know . . . yet. But, on the cusp of forty, I am listening to my dreams and daring to bare myself, my deepest passions, opinions, and hopes.

2

New Bones

Health, Beauty, and Self-Image

*Thirty years of monthly bleeding, PMS, cramps, pregnancy scares
and making the tampon manufacturers rich is enough. I'm not only
ready for menopause, I'm looking forward to it.*
— *Jill Nelson*, Straight, No Chaser: How
I Became a Grown-Up Black Woman

Age spots, thinning or graying hair, thickening waistlines, wrinkles, and sagging flesh are the most noticeable signs that we are getting older. They also can be the most painful as they are evidence that what many consider our currency — youth and its promise and beauty — is slipping away. In a society that values women mostly for our looks, the loss of them can be a terrible blow.

However, many sisters have *never* lived up to the dominant culture's ideas of beauty. Most of us have gotten the message that we are too "something": too heavy, too dark, too light, our noses too broad, our lips and thighs too thick. Mostly, we are deemed too "other." As mature women, let's let midlife liberate us from the tyranny of "the beauty myth" once and for all. Let's remind ourselves and our sisters that our worth runs much deeper than how we measure up to teenage supermodels. Our value lies in our brains and hearts, our strength, faith, courage, integrity, intelligence, humor, and compassion, *as well as* in our beauty. Because age does not preclude beauty, we can be older *and* lovely.

55

And healthy—if we take care of ourselves. Eating a healthy diet and getting plenty of exercise may ward off different types of cancers, heart disease, hypertension, diabetes, osteoporosis, and many other illnesses. Eat more fruits and vegetables and fewer fatty foods. Take long walks. Go out dancing. Play with your children or grandchildren. Do cartwheels. Twirl in circles. Have fun. As long as we're still kicking, let's kick!

It's also important to get regular checkups to monitor blood pressure and cholesterol levels and have annual mammograms, pap smears, colon cancer tests, and other health screenings. For health of mind and body, we must let go of resentments and past hurts and learn how to manage current stresses through meditation, prayer, yoga, or other relaxation techniques. Pampering is also an essential part of loving self-care. Indulge yourself with soothing baths, massages, facials, manicures, and pedicures.

Instead of lamenting our changing bodies, let's accept them, take care of them, and be grateful. Let's celebrate the beautiful bodies life has given us.

new bones

LUCILLE CLIFTON

we will wear
new bones again.
we will leave
these rainy days,
break out through
another mouth
into sun and honey time.
worlds buzz over us like bees,
we be splendid in new bones.
other people think they know
how long life is
how strong life is
we know.

Choosing Longevity

SUSAN L. TAYLOR

One Sunday I was sitting in Harlem's Abyssinian Baptist Church about half an hour before the eleven o'clock service was to begin. Because time is so precious, arriving before the beginning of service is rare for me. But *Essence* was celebrating an anniversary, and the pastor, the Reverend Calvin Butts, had invited me to speak about it at that Sunday's service and had asked me to arrive early. The elderly people were the first to enter the church. I watched them making their way to their seats. What a beautiful parade they were. They came with silver hair and Sunday hats. In suits and ties and in fellowship. They came alone and on one another's arms. Some aided by canes, one by a walker. You could easily see they were in varying states of health. *Which one of them will I be like in my elder years?* I wondered.

Since that Sunday, I've asked myself the questions we should ask often: how will I spend my later years? Will I be vital and independent, or will I be bent and feeble? Will I be mentally alert, engaged in life — or watching it from the sidelines? Will I even still *be* here? We all *want* to live healthy lives, but are we choosing longevity? Do our daily habits support or diminish our chances of aging well?

The generations before us didn't have the lifestyle choices we take for granted. Their lives were defined by hard work. When they were young, Hollywood glamorized smoking and drinking. Managing stress was unheard of. Our forebears inherited the delicious but unhealthy diets of their parents, and they paid the price. I don't want to suffer the strokes that killed my mother, my grandmother, and her mother, or the diabetes that took my father's life. I want to avoid the high blood pressure, the arthritis, and heart problems, the kidney and weight problems that limit the joy in so many of our elders' lives.

The lifestyle choices we make now will go a long way in determining if we are mentally alert, physically fit, and healthy in the autumn of our lives. When we're young and strong, it's hard to imagine ourselves otherwise. We take good health for granted. But good health is not preserved without constant, conscious effort.

While the larger population in this nation is living longer, the opposite is true for us. In our community, a shorter life span and physical debilitation affect the quality of life for more than just the individual. When we die young or are incapacitated, it means a loss of productivity that might otherwise help move our people forward. It saps the time and energy of those who have to care for us because we didn't care for ourselves. A vast amount of wisdom and life experience is lost to our children and generations to come when we fail ourselves.

We know what it takes to achieve longevity. Couch potatoes don't get there. Neither do folks who overeat or smoke or who drink too much or whose diets are high in fat, sugar, or salt. We can act from our power instead of from our weakness anytime we choose. You can be disciplined and committed—and must think of yourself as such. You are not inherently weak or inadequate; you are inherently strong. Your will is your most powerful tool. It's God mind in you. *"I will" are two of the most powerful words you can utter. Words that were in the beginning. Words through which the Creator created worlds. And all that is and ever shall be are but reverberations and repercussions of that first almighty thunderclap. I WILL. It is both a declaration and a command. It affirms dominion. Take a moment and whisper it to yourself. "I will." Feel the power.* Implicit in the words "I will" are the acknowledgment and affirmation that you have the power to choose. If you have the will to preserve your health, you can develop the will*power* that puts you in charge.

We are the parents of our elder selves. One of the most important decisions we must make at this time in our lives is to be better guardians of our health—for ourselves, for our children, and for our race.

Maneuvering through Menopause: A Rite of Passage

MARILYN HUGHES GASTON, M.D.,

AND

GAYLE K. PORTER, PSY.D.

Free at last! Free at last! Thank God Almighty we're free at last! That's exactly how so many of us feel after thirty or forty years enduring the discomfort, tension, and inconvenience of menstrual cycles. Like many of our friends, we couldn't wait to get off the rag. No more superabsorbent, superbig, or heavy-flow pads! No more superthin sanitary napkins with superabsorbent crystals that never "superabsorbed" anything. No more superabsorbent tampons that were never enough by themselves.

And best of all, no more cramps!

We couldn't wait. And all the while we remembered what we overheard our aunts, mothers, and grandmothers saying to one another when around the kitchen table: "Honey, I'm really, really starting to enjoy *it* since the change hit me and I don't have to worry about getting pregnant anymore." And they would all agree with a "Honey, hush!"

In truth, menopause is a bridge to the most vital and liberated period in a woman's life. It is a period of rebirth and positive change, a time to rediscover ourselves as spiritual and human beings with a long life ahead.

Midlife and menopause, its rite of passage, is a time of emotional and spiritual transformation. As our bodies and minds prepare for our later years, many women become more assertive, self-confident, and in touch with their own needs and wants, and less interested in pleasing others.

Unfortunately, not all of us celebrate our middle years. Many women buy into negative, stereotypical images and myths of midlife and menopause. Do any of these "menopause myths" sound familiar?

- Menopause will make me sick.

- I will lose my sexual desire during menopause—the light may be on, but the voltage is low.

- I will lose the hair on my head and instead grow hair on my face and chest.

- Menopause will make me fat.

Even though all women go through menopause, your experience will be uniquely your own. When it starts, when it stops, how we perceive it, and how it affects us varies from woman to woman—and it varies a lot. In fact, the menopause experience is so unique, some experts compare it to a thumbprint. For instance, although menopause may depress libido or sex drive in some women, many more report that sex is more satisfying and gratifying at this time in their lives than ever before. Even though the decrease in estrogen may thin the hair on the head of some women, statements of hair growth in unwanted places are being investigated. The one myth that does have some teeth may be weight gain. Your metabolism will slow down as you age, especially if you become more sedentary. That's why midlife women must get moving and keep moving—exercise is the key to health and to a healthy menopause. Watching your diet is also critical at this stage. You must eat less and improve the quality of what you eat. You can't afford to indulge yourself anymore with empty calories—you know, foods you love that are high in caloric content and very low in nutritional value, such as potato chips and ice cream.

On the other hand, the myth you should ignore altogether is that menopause will make you sick. Although you may experience some discomfort from hot flashes or lack of sleep, according to the National Institutes of Health, 80 percent of women experience mild or no menopausal signs at all. Only 20 percent report symptoms severe enough to require medical attention. Menopause is more than the end of monthly periods — it is a process and a journey during which many things happen. The important point to remember is that even though you don't have a choice about whether or not you go through menopause, *how* you respond to the experience is something you *can* control. To enjoy the journey, though, you must understand the changes taking place and how they affect your body, mind, and spirit. A typical American woman will live one-third of her life after menopause. Think about it — that could mean twenty-five to forty or more years without your period. Although there has been a tremendous increase in the amount of research on menopause in recent years, we still don't know a lot about it, and the existing studies haven't included an adequate number of African American women. Therefore, many important questions still remain unanswered, such as how much of the changes in our body are due to menopause or just to plain ol' aging.

Thankfully, the National Institute on Aging at the National Institutes of Health has initiated many investigations of menopause, estrogen, and the middle years, with adequate numbers of African American women, and soon we should have some important answers. In the meantime, though, we must go with what we know and be clear about what we don't know.

Menopause comes from the Latin words *meno*, meaning "month," and *pausus*, meaning "cessation," and literally means "the end of menstruation." Simply put, menopause is the time when your ovaries cease functioning and almost stop producing estrogen. This we know for sure. The average age for menopause in the United States and Canada is sometime between forty-five and fifty-five, usually around fifty-one. By sixty, virtually all women have experienced menopause. But remember, these average ages mean some women experience menopause much earlier, in their forties, and some much later, in their fifties and sixties. The onset of menopause is influenced by a number of factors. An important indicator is your mother's age when she began menopause. However, studies indicate that women who are less educated, poor, unemployed, or divorced and those who smoke tend to experience menopause somewhat earlier than average—maybe as much as three years earlier. Research attests that women who undergo early menopause—before age fifty—may be at greater risk for developing heart disease, osteoporosis (bone loss), and other chronic diseases.

Menopause is described in three phases: perimenopause, menopause, and postmenopause. *Perimenopause* usually means the years immediately *before* your last menstrual period. It usually begins in the mid- to late forties and can last from five to seven years.

Beginning as early as your mid- to late thirties, your ovaries start producing less estrogen and progesterone, even though you may continue to ovulate. Hormone levels fall even more dramatically when you enter perimenopause, which may happen as early as age thirty-five. Eventually, when the supply of viable eggs is exhausted, ovulation stops. At this time the levels of estrogen and progesterone produced by the ovaries drop so low that you stop menstruating all together.

One of the classic signs of perimenopause is *irregular menstrual cycles*. Before you stop menstruating, your periods may be longer or shorter, heavier, closer together, or farther apart. Even though this change is to be expected, *always report unusual bleeding to your doctor,* because irregular bleeding can also be a sign of fibroids, uterine polyps, a thyroid problem, or even cancer. If you are bleeding heavily, be sure to get a blood test to check for anemia, a condition in which the number of red blood cells (which carry oxygen) is below normal.

Since your body is starting to produce less estrogen during perimenopause, you may also start experiencing hot flashes, night sweats, vaginal dryness, mood swings, or depression.

Menopause is not official until you have not had a period for at least one year. But menopause includes a number of other physical, mental, and emotional changes.

Postmenopause represents the period after menopause. The lower levels of estrogen you have at this time can trigger "silent" changes in your body, including bone loss, which could lead to osteoporosis, and rising levels of bad (LDL) cholesterol coupled with a decrease in the good (HDL) in the blood. Over time, this can lead to heart attack and stroke.

Most women accept menopause in stride. It's important to think of menopause as a natural process, not an illness, sickness, or abnormal state. In fact, how you handle menopause may have a lot to do with your background. For example, Asian women report fewer and less severe signs than Western women, perhaps because for many Asian women menopause is a nonevent. In China, for instance, menopause is viewed as a good thing by both women and men, since age is venerated in Chinese culture. One study revealed that 65 percent of Japanese women reported no problems during menopause. The Japanese language does not even have a term for hot flashes. Only 2 percent of Japanese women take hormones.

Another significant reason for the difference in how Asian women handle menopause is dietary. Asian women eat great quantities of soybeans, which are extremely rich in isoflavones, a kind of phytoestrogen. These plant estrogens help balance the drop-off in our body's hormone levels during menopause. Asian women also consume more calcium, and they exercise (walking and biking daily) much more than we do. Their diet and exercise routines both pay healthy dividends, since Asian American women have the longest life expectancy—ninety-seven years!

Preliminary findings in a study being conducted by the National Institute on Aging (the Study of Women's Health Across the Nation, SWAN), which has a significant representation of African American women, indicates that Black women have more problems with hot flashes, night sweats, vaginal dryness, and urine leakage than other women. The study also shows that we have fewer headaches, problems with racing heartbeat, and stiffness and soreness in the joints, neck, or shoulders.

African American women are more likely than White women to pass through menopause without psychological problems. According to Gail Sheehy's survey of women in menopause reported in her book *New Passages: Mapping Your Life Across Time*, we may have an easier time with menopause than White women because:

• African American women tend not to measure our femininity and sensuality only by how we look.

• Young Black women usually have not been made to feel as valued as a symbol of beauty as young White women, and therefore are more prone to gain in prestige and self-esteem in middle age.

• Our self-worth is not overly attached to our age or to how young we look.

66

- Our sensuality is not related to the European American anorexic body type. (We know well the shamelessly lusty older Black women entertainers—from Della Reese to Patti LaBelle, from Jessye Norman to Etta James.)

The fact that Black women in midlife tend to be heavier than White women may also have a role in how we handle menopause. Estrogen is stored in fat, and, therefore, as our ovaries start producing less estrogen, our bodies use the estrogen in the body fat. The fact that we carry around more body fat means that we have more stored estrogen to use.

Although we've mentioned hot flashes, night sweats, and a few of the other signs of menopause, we haven't defined what happens when you experience any of these symptoms. Knowing what to expect can help ease you through the discomfort.

Hot Flashes and Night Sweats

Hot flashes are the most common signs of menopause. About 80 percent of menopausal American women experience hot flashes at some time. During a hot flash, your body temperature actually rises, the blood vessels in your skin dilate, the blood flow in your extremities increases, and you may appear flushed. Your heart rate goes up a little, maybe five to ten more beats a minute. Changes in estrogen can cause hot flashes. Some pregnant women also complain of flashing. Low estrogen levels affect the *hypothalamus* (your body's climate control center in the brain). A drop in estrogen upsets the ability of the hypothalamus to regulate your internal temperature. Triggers for hot flashes include spicy food, hot drinks, alcoholic drinks, white sugar, hot weather, hot tubs and saunas, tobacco and marijuana, stress, and anger, especially when unexpressed.

Night sweats are simply hot flashes that occur at night while you sleep, but they can sometimes be so severe that they prevent you from sleeping. If they lead to sleep deprivation, you should seek medical attention.

Prime-Time Prescriptions for Hot Flashes, Night Sweats, and Sleep Problems

- Add soy protein to your daily diet.

- Avoid all types of caffeinated drinks and foods, including coffee, tea, cola drinks, and chocolate.

- Avoid alcohol, sugary drinks or foods, spicy foods, hot soups, and very large meals.

- Take vitamin E. Studies show that 400 to 800 IU of vitamin E prevents hot flashes in some women.

- Increase your activity level.

- Reduce physical tension brought on by stress by deep breathing and massage.

- Stay hydrated by drinking eight to ten glasses of water a day.

- Keep cool.

- Meditate.

- Use special herbs in your cooking. Some herbs, such as ginseng, dong quai, and licorice root, have estrogenic properties and are often recommended for the discomforts of menopause. Be careful, though. *Do not use ginseng, dong quai, or licorice root if you have high blood pressure! Black cohosh* also has been well studied for its ability to chill out hot flashes. *Cohosh* is an Eastern Abenaki (Native American) word that means "knobby rough roots," and the Native Americans were the first to use black cohosh to treat female ailments. Mild side effects such as upset stomach, headache, dizziness, and weight gain have all been reported. The dose that works best seems to be a supplement capsule of 40 milligrams of root per day (larger doses may be unsafe) or drinking a tea made with the herb. Herbal and other natural and dietary remedies are increasingly popular for menopausal symptoms.

- Try herb teas to help you sleep.

- Consider acupuncture and biofeedback.

Vaginal Dryness

Decreased estrogen causes the walls of your vagina to become thinner, drier, and less elastic. The vaginal lining also pales and the vaginal tissues become increasingly fragile. As the vaginal tract becomes drier, sexual intercourse can become uncomfortable, even painful, and, consequently, your interest in sexual activity may diminish. Because vaginal dryness is often discussed as a symptom of menopause, women mistake this as a sign that their bodies are no longer interested in sex. You can have and enjoy sex as long as you live. If pain from vaginal dryness is a problem, you can find a healing remedy in the different hormonal creams. The dryness also causes itching and irritation and a tendency to develop repeated vaginal infections.

The bladder and urinary tract also can be affected by menopausal changes, and you may lose a little urine while laughing, coughing, or exercising. This condition is referred to as *stress incontinence*. Women suffering from this problem also find themselves running faster to get to the bathroom because they're unable to hold their urine as well as before.

Prime-Time Prescriptions for Vaginal Dryness

- Schedule a checkup with your doctor. Do not start any self-treatments before checking with your doctor so you can be sure any vaginal irritation is not due to an infection.

- Stop douching, if you are! Douching can irritate the vagina and make matters worse.

- Have more sex. Believe it or not, being sexually active helps. Sexual arousal increases the blood flow to the vaginal area and stimulates natural lubrication.

- Discuss with your doctor the pros and cons of taking estrogen.

to my last period

LUCILLE CLIFTON

well girl, goodbye,
after thirty-eight years.
thirty-eight years and you
never arrived
splendid in your red dress
without trouble for me
somewhere, somehow.

now it is done,
and i feel just like the grandmothers who,
after the hussy has gone,
sit holding her photograph
and sighing, *wasn't she
beautiful? wasn't she beautiful?*

Hair Matters at Midlife

BRENDA J. ALLEN

Since I've stopped dyeing my hair, more people than ever are calling me "ma'am." Salespeople even ask me if I'm eligible for a senior citizen discount. Though many people compliment my silver strands, others seem to view them simply as evidence of aging. I don't want to care about what people think about my hair and my age, but I do. While their opinions don't matter enough for me to change my mind about subsidizing Clairol, my hair story is as complex as the dynamics among race, gender, and sexuality.

My baby pictures show a round brown girl with a big old Charlie Brown head topped with a few wisps of hair. I was cute as a bald-headed button. My photo at four years of age portrays a little darlin' with a head full of hair, neatly plaited and beribboned.

When I was little, folks in the Youngstown, Ohio, projects where I grew up often complimented my long, coarse, thick, "Indian" hair. "Your hair is *so* pretty." "You got *good* hair." As always, though, Ma kept me levelheaded. "There's no such thing as 'good' hair," she would retort. About once a week, I would climb up on the kitchen sink and lie across the countertop for her to wash my hair. Sometimes she conditioned it with mayonnaise or egg yolks. One time she rinsed it with beer! I wanted her to use a straightening comb like my friends' mothers used on their hair, but she said I didn't need it. I can almost smell the Dixie Peach hair grease. On special occasions, Ma would use brown paper bag twists and bobby pins to set my hair in "Shirley Temple" curls. "Don't break your neck," she would caution as I shook my head to make my curls bounce.

I learned lots of lessons about hair from folks in my community. My friends and I had a running joke. A man asked a woman, "Did you use Madame Walker on your hair?" "Why, yes," she replied. "Well, Madame need to Walker around those nappy edges," he crowed. Good grooming meant having neatly pressed edges and a straight "kitchen." I never could figure out why they called the hair on your neckline the kitchen. A favorite comeback line when playing the dozens went like this: "You ain't got no mama; you got two baldheaded daddies." We would describe the shameful length of someone's hair with a simple snap of our fingers: "Her hair was" — snap! — "*that* short!"

I've had a small gray patch in the front of my hair (just like my grandpa) for as long as I can remember. An older man once remarked, "You too young to be worried about anything." Folks would say about a gray hair, "Don't pull it out, or two more will grow in."

My grandma had long, thick auburn hair that a lucky grandchild would scratch and grease whenever we visited her. We kids would fuss over who would get the honors. Superstition said it was bad luck for two people at a time to comb a person's hair. I guess that meant bad luck for the combee, not the combers.

By junior high, the only way I could tame my hair was to press it with a hot comb. After heating the comb on the gas flame of our stove, I would blow on it and wipe it on a cloth to cool it down. One time, a girl I know burnt her lip doing that. Ouch. I still remember the sizzling sound and stinging sensation of the comb meeting ear, neck, or forehead rather than hair. Thanks to technological progress, I could roll my hair in pink sponge curlers instead of the soft pink plastic ones that had replaced the paper bag twists. Sometimes I would go to the hairdresser to get my hair done, but usually Ma or I did it. Strangers would sometimes give me the dubious compliment that my hair looked like a wig. "It's so thick," they'd exclaim.

In high school, some of my friends and I experimented with

coloring our hair. Our favorite shade was Sparkling Sherry, a pretty brownish red color. Once I even used pure peroxide to make a blonde streak. For my high school photo, I had my hair done in a flip, like Florence Ballard in the Supremes. I just knew that I looked "tuff." Through my high school years, I wore a beehive, a pageboy, a ball, and a French twist. Sometimes I would wear a headband that matched my outfit.

During my second year in college, I managed to frizz my hair into a hee-yuge Angela Davis afro. I would wash, braid, roll, and air-dry it. After taking out the curlers, I'd pick it out and cover it lightly with a chiffon scarf to mold it into shape. Later I would use Afro Sheen to give it a serious gloss. With my long legs, big 'fro, blue-tint granny glasses, and tie-dyed jeans, it was hard to tell if I was female or male. Once, while waiting for the Greyhound bus to take me from Cleveland to Youngstown on spring break, I overheard one man ask another, "Is that a man or a woman?" That wouldn't be the last time that someone would question my gender or sexuality because of my hair.

When I got home, Ma was appalled by my bushy look. To get it shaped up, I went to an older barber who had no experience at all with the brand-new style. He clipped and he mowed, and he trimmed my hair down to about two inches. Although I saw hair piling up on the floor, I didn't expect to see the image that the mirror he held in front of me displayed. This would be the first of many disappointing visits to barber and beauty shops. When Ma came to pick me up, I boo-hooed all the way home. I was devastated. But when my friends told me that I looked sharp, I grew to love my tiny 'fro. I was hip! I was cool! Older folks didn't like it, though. "Why in the world did you cut your hair, child?" "You done cut off your glory," moaned one of my aunts. "People trying to grow hair, and here you go cutting yours." I wore my afro until I finished college, then I moved on to other styles. Ma ended up wearing a natural for years.

For a while in graduate school, I parted my hair on the side or down the middle and French braided my hair in one long coil that I'd pin up in the back. Then I started using relaxers, which meant I had to roll my hair up almost every night. And I had to get touch-ups on a regular basis. I fluctuated between wearing it longish or short. I hated that in-between time when I was trying to grow it long. More than a few times, I grew impatient. I'd wake up one day and decide that I couldn't stand it any longer. Off I'd go to get it chopped off again.

One overcast day in D.C., I boarded the bus to work wearing a long trench coat. My hair was long, freshly permed (actually it was relaxed), and looking fine, fine, fine. As I sat down near the front, I heard snickering from the back. Accustomed to youthful enthusiasm, I ignored it. Then I realized that I was the object of derision. "Look at that faggot wearing a wig," one of the young teenaged boys shrieked, as the others cracked up laughing. Another one called out, "Take off that big wig, faggot." Everyone else on the bus ignored them. I tried to, but their misperception disturbed me. When the bus got to my stop, I stepped to the back door, even though I was closer to the front. I wanted the young brothers to get a good look at me and realize their mistake. As I got closer, their eyes widened as realization dawned. Acting oblivious to them, I stepped off the bus. I was as ashamed of wanting to deny I was a gay man as I was embarrassed that they thought I was.

In my late thirties, more and more gray started coming in. I started coloring my hair every three weeks or so. Around seven years ago, as I guided workshop participants through a self-empowerment meditation, I envisioned myself with sparkling silver hair. However, I didn't think more about that image until I decided

on a whim not to dye my hair. In October 1997, my dear friend
Frances succumbed to cancer. Fran's beautiful hair had fallen out
after chemotherapy. "I look like a cancer patient," she remarked in
that dry way of hers as she viewed a videotape of herself. I made an
emergency appointment to get my hair done before I traveled from
Colorado to D.C. to Fran's funeral. As my stylist prepared to do my
hair, I expressed frustration at needing to color it again so soon. I
hated for my roots to show, and my hair grows so quickly that the
gray seemed to sprout out within days, right in the front of my head.
(One time I used one of those pencils to draw in some color. Now
that looked real stupid.) "Well," he said, "I can cut it down to the
gray to see how it looks." Hmmm, I thought. Why not try it. If I
didn't like it, I could always dye it. And Fran always liked my hair
short. Let's try it. He had to cut it real short—shorter than I could
ever remember wearing it. The results were fabulous. I'm sure that
Fran would have loved my new look!

Although I've had a lifetime of black folks commenting on my
hair, I wasn't ready for what would happen once I went gray. Several people I know asked me if I got it frosted or streaked. The man
I was dating told me that I looked ten years younger (which means
I looked about his age). Brothers I don't even know often tell me
how much they love it, which surprises me because I thought black
men loved them some hair. One even told me that he admired my
courage to just be me. Sisters compliment me, too. Younger ones
say things like, "I can't wait for mine to grow in," or "Ma'am, your
hair is beautiful." Those closer to my age are more expressive:
"Ooooh, your hair is *gorgeous!*" Or they bemoan their felt need to
keep coloring: "Mine doesn't look as nice as yours." "Hmph, I'm
dyeing mine," said one woman after her friend complimented me.

Last year, I got a new job. After four years of not coloring my hair,
I yielded to momentary insecurity and dyed my hair dark brown.
I left a patch of gray in front to resemble my earlier years. Almost

immediately, I regretted it. The color was harsh and the patch looked phony. Damn. I would just have to wait until my hair grew long enough to cut it back down. As soon as it was long enough, I had my hair cut down to the gray. Yesss. That's more like it.

Once in a while, I dream that my hair is long and dark again. The other night, I even dreamed of wearing a wig. Those nocturnal visions don't faze me, though. I know that gray hair signifies aging, and it should in my case since I'm not getting younger. But I am getting better. Call me "ma'am" all you want. I know that salt and pepper means spicy. As they say, "There may be snow on the rooftop, but there's still fire in the furnace."

I'm proud of myself for going back to my roots. I keep my hair cut short, not because they say that older women don't look good with long hair, but because I like the way it looks. Plus, it's easier to maintain. I'm glad to be alive and dealing with no signs of midlife other than graying hair (well, every now and then I have a hot flash, er, power surge). Now that's a blessing. I love my silver, and I plan to keep it. In a few years, when someone asks if I'm eligible for a senior discount, I will gladly reply, "Yes, thank you!"

Am I Ugly?

TERRI SUTTON

It was Tuesday, my regular day to pick up my nine-year-old niece from school. This was a routine I'd started when Myesha was still in day care, a guarantee of spending at least one afternoon a week with her. Over the years, the basics of our afternoons had changed only slightly. There was food, talk, and an activity we could do together. When Myesha was younger, the activity was usually snuggling on the couch, where I would read to her until she drifted off into a nap. In more recent years, our activity time had led me to explore the woody trails of my neighborhood park and, after much practice, to learn the latest clapping games that girls invariably perform on playgrounds.

Myesha and a girl I recognized as one of her friends strolled toward the parking lot, whispering back and forth to each other. In front of my car, they parted—waving with the wild abandon that only children can muster. Myesha pulled the door open and in one efficient motion flung her Barbie book bag into the car then hopped into the backseat.

I heard the clinking of the barrettes that dangled from the ends of her braids. She thumped the back of the passenger seat with her tennis shoe. She's tall like her dad. "Seat belt," I reminded before shifting into gear to leave the lot. It was a reflex, not a required prompting. She fastened, and when I looked back, she was staring out the side window, her head tilted upward at the sky.

"Can I ask you something?" she said, moments later as I pulled into the McDonald's drive-thru.

"Sure," I said.

She was silent for a few seconds, long enough for me to hear her sudden intake of air, then a steady exhale. "Am I ugly?"

Experience has taught me that for certain questions it's the time it takes to supply the answer that carries more importance than the answer itself. And so I responded quickly, "No, Myesha. You're not ugly."

When I glanced in the rearview mirror, I expected to see her deep-dimpled grin that would tell me she was teasing or that solemn look of satisfaction she got whenever I told her exactly what she needed to hear. But instead her face appeared frozen still, her eyes narrowed as if she was examining a priceless coin.

"Why do you ask?" I said.

She hesitated, and it seemed to me the first time Myesha had been reluctant to speak her mind.

"There's a boy," she said. "I like him, but he doesn't like me." She dragged one French fry through a glob of ketchup.

"Who is this boy?" I asked, already picturing a cruel, little oaf in my mind.

After swearing me to secrecy, she revealed his name. "He's nice," she said, "but I want him to like me."

"There's a lot that goes into liking someone," I said, emphasizing *a lot*. "You can't really explain what makes one person like another. . . ."

She stopped me. "No," she said. "It's happened before." She was watching me now—leaning forward the way she did when one of her favorite songs came on the radio. "At my last school. I liked a boy . . . but . . . he didn't like me back, so I was thinking maybe it's because I'm ugly."

At that moment, I knew I couldn't explain the mysterious path that leads to an attraction for one person, but not another. Instead, I crafted examples about the subtleties of preferences: jeans—straight-legged or flared—and hairstyles—braided or pony-tailed. With each instance, I talked faster, like a rapid-firing pistol. I moved on to games, followed by movies, snacks, teachers, girl-

79

friends, then finally I drew comparisons with boy-girl relationships. I wanted to give Myesha more than ugliness to think about,
to overwhelm her with other possibilities. I didn't want her to con-
clude that she was ugly because she couldn't think of anything
else.

"We like people for all sorts of reasons not connected to how
they look," I said. "It might be the way they laugh . . . or because
they like the same things you do . . . or because of how smart the
person is." I caught a glimpse of her in the mirror. "Does that make
sense?"

She shrugged, but I could tell she was thinking about what I'd
said—she's that kind of child. And I was thinking, too, about ugliness and a picture of myself years ago when I was thirteen.

I don't remember the occasion when the picture was taken. In
those days, any Sunday afternoon might find my sister, brother,
and me in the backyard still dressed from church while my mother
snapped photos of us with the Instamatic camera. What I do recall
is that I liked the picture of me standing in the backyard, wearing
a lime green dress with a white leather belt that showed off my
small waist. I was posed in the way girls did then—arms behind me,
my head tilted to one side, and with just enough sway in my hips
to suggest a promising body.

One day, my brother suddenly materialized while I sat at the
kitchen table admiring the photo. At sixteen, he was constantly in
motion, sweeping through the house on his way to meet friends or
to get to football practice. But this day, he paused long enough to
peer over my shoulder at the picture.

"Look at old, ugly Terri," he said, then disappeared out the side
door.

If he had said it in the taunting way that older brothers usually
talk to baby sisters, I would have responded in kind and then forgotten about it. But his tone had been amicable and so matter-of-

fact that he could have been making an observation about the weather. Even my mother, who was busy in the kitchen, said nothing—not even the usual, "You know better than that," her familiar reprimand for our minor infractions. It was as if my brother's declaration of my ugliness was such an obvious truth that it had, by tacit agreement, gone unsaid for the first thirteen years of my life.

After that, I was changed. In retrospect, it seems absurd that a few careless words should have affected me so deeply, but from that day something that I'd never considered before became a permanent part of me. Don't misunderstand, like other girls my age I had compared myself to the competition, and, to the extent that one can, I'd given myself an honest assessment. Maybe this one had nicer hair (that was important then . . . and perhaps now, too) or that one wore better clothes or had a better figure. Until that day, my appraisal had been that I was comfortably situated in the mid-range—not a candidate for a circus freak show or a beauty contest.

I considered the standards of beauty for African American women. There was Lena Horne, an indisputably exquisite-looking woman, with keen features, straight hair, and thin lips. Today we don't talk about the preference of having European traits but back then we all knew it was better to have hair "like white people." Diahann Carroll, star of *Julia*, had a polished style beyond anything I could attain while locked in the bathroom and experimenting with drugstore makeup. When I compared myself to these women, I felt the full weight of my ugliness—a skinny, yellow-skinned girl with nappy hair.

I settled into the life of an ugly girl. I became quiet and shy. My insecurity about my appearance led me to avoid anything that might draw attention to myself because that would invite people to see old, ugly Terri. I understood when my friends and I went out that boys and later men would be more interested in my attractive friends. I believed that any attention I received was a gesture of pity or boredom and accepted practically all dates because I assumed the invitations would be few and far between. Once when I was in high school, I dated a boy who, in plain terms, I loathed. He never listened to anything I said, opting instead to interrupt or "talk over" me. On those occasions when we ate out, he would stuff hamburgers and onion rings in his mouth, then chew through a conversation. At times I was so disgusted by the sight of his eating that I would excuse myself to the ladies room just to get away. And yet, I never refused his invitations.

My accepted ugliness undermined every aspect of my life. As an adult, I became a pleaser, believing my acquiescence was a necessary concession. I doubted the motives of every relationship. Why would any man be attracted to me? Why would any woman want to be my friend? While most girls wanted to squeeze into the smallest dress size possible, I deliberately bought clothes a size larger than I needed. My goal was to camouflage my ugly body as expertly as I camouflaged my inner self.

Then one day I realized that soon I would be fifty. Although I had always exercised regularly and followed a careful diet, I couldn't stop the spreading cellulite on my thighs or the hanging flab on my arms. My body was changing. I acknowledged that the Lena-and-Diahann ideals no longer seemed applicable—or enviable to me. This realization had an oddly jarring effect on me. While I felt a sense of relief at not having the unattainable overshadowing me, I also felt a sense of loss. Where were my standards of beauty?

At the same time, I was preoccupied with questions. Who defined ugliness? Did I have to accept that definition? What was I really like? Did I respect myself? Would I want myself as a friend? Was I living the life I wanted? For these questions, I had few answers. Equally disturbing was my growing annoyance with people, accustomed to my compliancy, who continually made demands of me, and I was irritated with myself when I gave in. "That's what happens when you turn fifty," my mother told me when I complained about their insensitivity. "You just won't tolerate people messing with you." I wondered if she was right. Maybe fifty was the gateway to intolerance. Increasingly dissatisfied with myself and unwilling to remain in the role I had played for so many years, I decided it was time to examine another picture.

I was the only one who saw this imaginary photo of me sitting in an orange velour chair, a gift from my sister when I moved to Wisconsin in 1983. Though I donated this chair to Goodwill years ago, I invented a snapshot of myself, pressed into its comfortable, buttoned back, hands folded in my lap. Deliberately, I brought neither my face nor my body into sharp focus, sensing that I didn't need to see what was outside, I needed to concentrate on what was inside.

For months I studied my photo, always in the chair although sometimes posed with my legs curled under me or leaning on an armrest, reminding me of *The Thinker*. I searched for clues to understand the life I'd led. Like a detective, I followed the threads back through critical moments when this response instead of that might have made a difference. I returned to that day in the kitchen when my brother had casually defined me as ugly. Each time I remembered, I imagined another way to counter him. "Who asked you?" I might have said, or "It takes one to know one." Even rolling my eyes in smoldering defiance would have been better than accepting his pronouncement. Thinking about the power I'd given his words embarrassed me.

In time I began reading self-discovery books, searching for explanations for my behavior. There was no shortage of works that were loaded with theories, case studies, key agreements, spiritual laws, and makeovers to help me analyze my life. I devoured them all, reveling in the range of possibilities and solutions they represented. Finally, I had the power to define my past and to shape my future.

On some days, changing was difficult, and other days it seemed impossible. Backsliding into comfortable, painful habits was easier than cultivating new ones. Frequently after agreeing to something I didn't want to do, I would force myself to renege, explaining tactfully and sometimes timidly to the person that I couldn't comply. With practice, it became easier for me to say "no" immediately to acquaintances and colleagues when their requests were counter to my own needs. And any feelings of fear or insecurity that I'd experienced in the past began to fade. Last year, ignoring all skepticism, I went back to school to fulfill a dream of studying writing.

Since then, I measure myself by what I see in my imaginary picture. I focus on what I am learning, by the people I am affecting in a positive way, and by what I am giving to my community. Every day I meditate to get in touch with the inner person that I am, and I don't consider how that person looks to others because I know she is beautiful to me.

The next Tuesday I picked up Myesha as usual. After talking to her about school, her food preference, and giving the "seat belt" reminder, I mentioned the boy that she had talked about the week before. "Any changes?" I asked.

"No," she said, pursing her lips. "That's just the way he is."

Banyan Trunk

ADA NELRIBI

Sister, sister how long has it been?
Through cornrows, dreads,
through literal thick and thin
we've grown with time and place.

Like the echo off concrete, the snap of a jump rope
replaced by the boom box beat
and now our offspring speak songs.

We have become calmer women.
Our anger no long even simmers,
a cooler porridge heals hard times,
distant the troubles we have traversed.

With the few inches and
with the few pounds, we, sister,
have gained a quiet, steady wisdom.
Clear in cadence and timber.

Banyan trees grow substantial
by the Nile River and we, sister,
have trunks both thick and graceful,
roots as sure as gravity itself.

from *I Left My Back Door Open*

APRIL SINCLAIR

I am not young, or thin, or white, or beautiful. I'm a slightly thick sista, but I know how to fix myself up. And I'm on the radio. My name is Daphne Dupree, and I play the blues.

I liked everything about speaking into a mike. I even enjoyed positioning my mouth in front of one. And I loved the way my voice sounded, so rich and full, when it came out. Maybe I just liked to hear myself talk.

"We opened the set with the incomparable Etta 'Miss Peaches' James doing 'At Last.' That was by special request from Dianne, a blue-eyed soul sister who knows that when you make a potato salad, you don't leave out the mustard.

"Speaking of food, we're gonna be broadcasting live from Taste of Chicago, in Grant Park next Saturday. I hope to see some of my listeners. You know I'm gon' sho' 'nuff be tastin', too. 'Cause, honey, there's no such thang as a black anorexic!" I laughed. "You heard it here first."

I kept right on b.s.in', 'cause I was on a roll. And I was in control. "Y'all remember, last year, my boyfriend didn't hit me, but he up and quit me? Yeah, he said, 'Dee Dee you too big,' sho' did. The brotha didn't 'preciate my meat. He wasn't no natchel man. Finally had to tell 'im, I was built for comfort, not for speed!"

I paused for air. "You know, it's funny, there was a time when a skinny woman was almost looked at as deformed. She damn near had to run away and join the circus." I sighed. "When I was a child, nobody wanted the woman with the skinny legs. And don't let her have the nerve to be flat-chested, with no booty, too. You had to have something to shake back in them days."

86

I noticed a lighted button. "I got a call coming in on the board. Somebody out there must be feeling my pain."

"Girlfriend, you need to come on back home to the soulful South Side," the voice on the line urged.

"It sounds like my friend, Sarita."

"Yeah, it's me, girl. Anyway, it's plenty of men on the South Side who like full-figured women."

"Sista, you say I'm just dealing on the wrong side of town? You think that's what it is?"

"I know that's what it is. You drive around the South Side, and you see big behinds everywhere. And it ain't keeping nobody from getting no man, or putting on no pair of shorts, either."

"Big behinds are all over the North Side, too," I insisted. "You need to get out more. Big behinds are everywhere now, and they come in all colors. And they're coming to a theater near you."

"Girl, you crazy! We don't have no theaters around here. I'm calling you from the 'hood."

"It was just an expression."

"Anyway, Dee Dee, you need to come on back to church, 'cause, honey, there're plenty of women heavier than you. In fact, they'd run and bring you a plate of food, girlfriend. Try to fatten you up."

"All right, I'll be in your church on Sunday. So save me some pew. And give some sugar to my play nephew. I just can't help but rhyme, almost every time."

"Okay, then, you put on Koko Taylor for your good girlfriend."

"A request for the reigning Queen of the Blues is always good news! But, first, it's time for the tips, and I'll shoot 'em from the hips. If you want your holiday to be a blast, when you barbecue, put your sauce on last. You can baste it with vinegar, you can baste it with beer. But, Koko fixin' to pitch a 'Wang Dang Doodle,' then I'm outta here! That concludes this edition of Deep Dish Blues on

WLUV, 98.6 on your FM dial. And I'm your hostess with the mostest, Dee Dee Joy, born in Alabama and raised in Illinois."

I'd taken off my headphones and unglued my hips from the one-size-don't-fit-all swivel chair. Jade was at the mike now. I listened to her sultry voice as I sauntered through the air-conditioned state-of-the-art studio on Chicago's waterfront.

"Welcome to the world of Belly," Jade said mysteriously, in her Chinese accent. "Slip on your finger cymbals. Toreador your veils. Put your camels to bed. We've got two hours of Egyptian pop ahead."

I swayed to the beat as I entered the spacious but deserted reception area. My ears were filled with the moaning of Egyptians, but my eyes were drawn to the view of the cluster of boats navigating the lake. Outside the picture windows, people strolled along the water's edge or sat in open-air cafes. On summer nights like this one, a jazz band played below a Budweiser sign. Navy Pier was a tourist attraction, pure and simple. But I admired the colorful Ferris wheel lit up against the darkening sky.

Suddenly, I felt someone's presence, and my body jumped. I turned around. It was Rob, the station manager. He looked like Mike Moore, the guy who made the movie *Roger and Me.*

"I didn't mean to startle you," Rob said, apologetically.

"I didn't know you were still here," I answered.

"Yeah, I'm still pushing papers," Rob sighed. "Anyway, I got your memo," he continued. "But, guess what, you don't have to worry about doing that stinking fund-raiser this year, you're off the damn hook."

"I didn't mind doing it," I answered. "It was for a good cause. Besides, I can think of worse things than emceeing an event at the Four Seasons. Plus, they've always requested me."

"Yeah, and all these years you've been a trouper." Rob patted me on the shoulder.

"Well, what happened?" I asked, confused. "Have they decided not to do it this year? It was always so successful."

"They're still gonna do it, all right," Rob assured me. "But this year they just decided to try a different angle, go after a different crowd."

"A different crowd?" I asked, wrinkling my forehead.

"Yeah, a younger bunch."

"How young?"

"I don't know, I guess twenties and thirties."

"Rob, I'm in that age range, more or less," I said trying to sound calm.

"How old are you now, Dee Dee, thirty-nine?"

I swallowed. "Close, I just turned forty-one."

"Ouch, I thought we were the same age. Damn, you're getting up there."

I sighed. "It's not that serious."

"You're right. You've got quite a few years left before you'll need dentures. By the way, happy belated birthday."

"Thanks. So, who are you going to get to do the fund-raiser?" I asked, turning and staring out the window again.

"I'm gonna run it by Jennifer."

"Jennifer!" I wheeled back around. "But she's just an intern!"

"Yeah, but she's bright and perky. Really perky," Rob added, making animated gestures. "I think that's the type they're looking for."

"What am I, iron-tired blood?" I asked, rolling my eyes.

"Not at all. You did a great job all these years. Everyone says that. They just want to appeal to the damn yuppies, you know, Wicker Park, Lincoln Park. . . ."

"Bucktown," I added.

"Yeah, exactly, those types. You understand."

"Yeah, I guess," I said, trying to sound like a team player.

89

"Good. By the way, your show was great as always. Now, go home and put your feet up."

That's not what you would tell Jennifer, I thought. *You would tell her to party like it's 1999.*

I pressed the button for the elevator. When I was a child, forty seemed older than God. I could more easily imagine myself dying in a car crash at thirty-nine than living to see forty.

But, somehow, I had managed to reach forty. And as if that hadn't been traumatic enough, last week, I turned forty-one. Nobody told me that forty was just a dress rehearsal for forty-one. Now I was *in* my forties. And a whole decade was harder to deny than a measly year. I stepped into the empty elevator. At least on my last birthday, I still had a boyfriend. Now I was all alone, except for my cat.

Used

RITA DOVE

The conspiracy's to make us thin. Size threes
are all the rage, and skirts ballooning above twinkling knees
are every man-child's preadolescent dream.
Tabula rasa. No slate's *that* clean—

we've earned the navels sunk in grief
when the last child emptied us of their brief
interior light. Our muscles say *We have been used.*

Have you ever tried silk sheets? I did,
persuaded by postnatal dread
and a Macy's clerk to bargain for more zip.
We couldn't hang on, slipped
to the floor and by morning the quilts
had slid off, too. Enough of guilt—
It's hard work staying cool.

My Cups Used to Runneth Over

DIANE DONALDSON

African American women and cosmetic surgery sounds like an oxymoron, doesn't it? Not. Not with breasts so heavy you have to wear an industrial-strength bra, which digs into your skin. Not with excruciating back pain. Thank God I was able to reduce my breasts from a DDD cup to a "full C cup." The surgery was worth every penny, every pain, and every scar. And I don't mind mentioning the added benefit of having perky breasts as I near forty years old. While other women complain about how their breasts sag and how they have to wear a bra all the time, I smile smugly and say, "I don't. Ever since I had my boobs reduced, I stay in the same place. I don't even have to wear a bra—only a tube top!" Rolled eyeballs and envy always follow my declaration. I love it!

I've been well endowed since I was ten and filled a C cup. By the time I turned thirty, I wore a DD cup. Growth didn't stop there. At thirty-five, I breast-fed my son for his first year, and I blossomed to a DDD cup. After I weaned him, for several months I kept waiting for my breasts to return to "normal" size. I waited a few months more. Nothing. I thought, "Oh, that's right. I haven't lost my pregnancy weight." So, I started an exercise program and began a low-fat diet and lost thirty pounds, but my breast size remained the same. Finally, by age thirty-eight, I became disenchanted with the large-breasted-hey-guys-I'm-up-here drama. I also couldn't go to my local department store to purchase a bra—my size was only available through catalogs (only in the "fashionable" colors of white and beige) and I had to pay over thirty dollars per bra.

After my breast-reduction surgery, I cheered, "No more big-breasted specialty catalogs—yippee! I'm free." Why would anyone who was so well endowed reduce what other women pay to enhance? Why, indeed. Let me give several reasons:

- I couldn't lie on my stomach without feeling like I was lying on two Rocky Mountains.

- When I lay on my back, my breasts would cascade down each side of my body and almost (yikes!) touch the mattress.

- I experienced shoulder and back pain.

- My breasts were so heavy and pulled the bra straps so tight that the straps left indentations, grooves, and dark lines in the skin of my shoulders and back.

- I experienced mega amounts of sweat under each breast, which led to athlete's foot fungus (yes, foot fungus) on my areolas.

- When standing, even with a bra on, my breasts were so large and pendulous that they hung close to my waist and seemed to merge with my stomach, making it look as if I were pregnant.

- For clothing purposes, my top half didn't match my bottom half. I was 3X at the top and XL at the bottom. Now I'm XL and XL. Beautiful. I haven't experienced a matching top and bottom since eighth grade.

Now, before anyone goes and schedules an appointment with the nearest plastic surgeon, let me advise that breast-reduction surgery or reduction mammaplasty is no picnic. It was painful, and it takes months before you feel fully recovered. Scars are permanent; some keloiding may develop, which makes for dark and unattractive scars. For the first week after my surgery, I needed assistance going to the bathroom, changing my bandages, and putting on my chest binder. Sleeping in a recliner was easier and preferable to a bed.

My surgeon used the most common reduction mammaplasty method. It started with a three-part incision. One part of the incision was made around the nipple area. Another incision ran vertically from the bottom edge of the areola to the crease underneath the breast. The third part included a horizontal incision beneath the breast, which followed the natural curve of my breast crease. After the surgeon removed the excess breast tissue, fat, and skin, the nipple and the areola were shifted to a higher position (so my nipples point straight ahead instead of pointing toward the ground) and the areola reduced. Skin located above the nipple was brought down, then together, to reshape the breast. Since very little fatty tissue existed in my breasts, I did not need any liposuction. My nipples remained attached to their blood supply and underlying tissue so I still have feeling in my breasts and nipples. My surgery was so successful and I gave such rave reviews that my older sister, at age forty-six, also had her breasts reduced, and my mother's friend, who is fifty and a mother of four, also had her breasts reduced, lifted, and "lipoed." My sister and my mother's friend also elected to have a five-day radiation treatment after surgery to help eliminate keloiding.

The reduction surgery has taken years and weight off all three of us, making us more energetic, more apt to exercise, and more self-confident instead of self-conscious. I look good in my clothes and can buy the bras for five dollars at the discount stores. Next to having a child at thirty-five, having reduction mammaplasty was one of the best decisions I've made. While I'm not a doctor or medical expert, I would recommend the procedure to any woman with large breasts who experiences shoulder or back pain or feels self-conscious about her appearance.

Please know that my breast-reduction surgery was not a decision I made lightly or quickly. It took me about a year of research and courage-building pep talks before I actually had the surgery performed. First, I consulted with my family physician, asking him for a plastic surgeon referral. Then, I interviewed two female coworkers about their reduction mammaplasty operations and discovered that six other women, all African American except one, had reduction surgery.

In addition, I consulted with my plastic surgeon twice. During my first visit, my breasts were photographed for insurance and before-and-after photo-file purposes. We discussed payment options along with which insurance plans and insurance companies would pay for reduction mammaplasty. Because my employer negotiated bare minimum benefits with its insurance provider, my HMO was only willing to cover breast surgery if it was related to breast cancer. However, during my company's open enrollment, I switched to a preferred provider organization (PPO), and my PPO covered all associated medical bills except for the deductible and the out-of-pocket maximum, which together amounted to seven hundred dollars. The hospital and the cosmetic surgeon's business office allowed me to make installment payments on the remaining balances.

After eight months of soul searching (and my niece agreeing to baby-sit my young son for a week), I scheduled the surgery. I felt apprehensive every day and almost backed out. But looking at those large "crumb catchers" hanging almost to my waist, and thinking of the time when a female coworker told me her eight-year-old daughter looked at her topless and said, "Mommy, you have looong boobies!" I couldn't cancel. I bravely walked into the hospital, allowed the plastic surgeon to draw lines on me with a black felt-tipped pen, let the nurse insert an IV in the side vein of my right hand, and then watched her as she shot me up with painkillers, nausea-preventing medication, and tranquilizers. Gulp. No turning back.

I awoke and looked down. *Yep. They're gone, now where's the nurse with my pain medication? I would hate for the morphine I received during surgery to wear off before getting my pain-dulling drugs.* Fortunately, the plastic surgeon that performed my surgery believes in "extended outpatient surgery," which means I wasn't kicked out of the hospital after waking from surgery—like my two coworkers were. I spent the night in the hospital recovering, allowing the nurses to take care of me.

I was sent home the next day with a list of instructions: no driving, sleep at a thirty-degree angle (to help the oozing), no lifting, no stretching, no bending or twisting, and change the gauze once a day. And I could shower, but I thought, "Why bother when I can't bend or twist to wash anything important," and my breasts hurt just by removing the binder.

Did I mention the horrific drive home? Even though I had on a breast-binding device, my surgically altered breasts felt every bump, pothole, and crack in every street. The drive took approximately forty minutes, and by the time I walked through the door, I felt death had to be near. "Why did I have this surgery?" I wondered again.

My son was up and about, acting like a normal two-year-old—jumping, laughing, and standing on his dad's shoulders. He became excited as I walked through the door. I fully expected him to run and jump on me. I braced myself for more excruciating pain. At that moment, my niece walked into the house with some balloons. I was saved; the balloons and my niece were his first choice. Whew.

I was in pain and uncomfortable, so I popped a couple of pain pills then settled in the bed and fell asleep. When I awoke, I heard my son say, "Momma's sick?" and he ran into my room, looked at me, and then ran back out. I also noticed the recliner had been put into the bedroom. Showering consisted of squirting some shower gel over parts I could reach and then letting the water run over my body. I changed into clean pajamas and then went into the kitchen to see if my mother or sister would help me change my bandages and close my chest binder. They were sitting at the table eating the chocolate cake my mother just bought.

"Oh, my God," my mother exclaimed. "You're so flat! She took too much! What *are* you going to do with those homemade boobs?" If her comment and facial expression weren't so funny, I would have been hurt. But as my best friend says, "A C cup is only flat compared to the women in your family."

For a short period, and because I was "known" for my large bust, I felt a little twinge of sadness when looking at the reduced "girls." However, after a year of not having back or shoulder pain and of having the grooves and dark lines in my shoulders disappear, I don't miss the notoriety or the large breasts at all. My year anniversary has come and gone and I still don't regret my decision. My breasts are high, happy, and normal-sized, and my shoulders don't ache from carrying around an extra five pounds of breast tissue. As a matter of fact, sometimes I think, "I wonder what my cosmetic surgeon could do about these thighs. . . ."

Middle-Age UFO

COLLEEN McELROY

The aliens have taken over
My body or else how
Could my head become suddenly
Medicine-ball heavy
Their ray-gun zap has left
Me old before my time
My joints so stiff and achy
I could easily teach a course
In robot behavior

Hot flash—night sweat
Is this Uranus or Neptune
There must be aliens
I hear them as they leave their ship
Yelling, "Men'o Pause, Advance!"
They must be males
They make their monthly raids
For female slaves
And what few men they take
Are quickly peeled like wounded
Onions down to their mushy centers
Women require years
First they fatten us in unlikely places
Until stomach and hips sag into gravity
They mean to change our lives
They want our secrets for having babies
But my lips are sealed

I follow a host of sisters and clutching
Passion, bailout
I quit that job — I'm out of here
I'm free to go on living

3

Roots

Family and Friendship

Although I am still in the midst of the confusion attendant to letting go of old situations and unsure of what direction I will take, I feel calm and happy in the love and support of my sisters.
—*Marilyn Hill Harper,* Wearing Purple

In the middle of our lives we reconsider our place in the human family tree. Our ancestors are the roots that link us to the earth, and our children are the branches that connect us to the heavens.

We reflect on the generations that have come before us and come to understand how they shaped us. We give thanks for the gifts we've received from our mothers, fathers, grandmothers, and grandfathers. And when we remember their faults, we forgive them for being less than the pillars of perfection we thought they should have been when we were younger. Now we know better. We have lived long enough to know that we all do the best we can, and when we can do better, we do.

We look at the generations that follow us and wonder how we have affected them. We give thanks for the gifts we've received from our children and grandchildren, praying that we've blazed a clear enough path for them to follow. And when we consider our faults, we forgive ourselves for not being the perfect role models that we had hoped to be.

In midlife, maybe more than ever, we value our connections to one another. Not only blood ties that bind us to generations, but emotional ties that join us with lovers, partners, and friends. Those who have saved our lives during times of stress, illness, and loss. Those who can make us laugh until we cry, and yet are brave enough not to require that we smile when we need to howl.

In this stage of our lives, we also know the poignancy of endings. Children grow up and leave home. Marriages dissolve; mates pass on. Friendships languish. Even when we don't want to, sometimes we have to let go. And yet in the letting go, we can rediscover ourselves. Our inner spirits. The long lost Selves we had abandoned to take care of everyone else.

In the middle of our lives we deeply understand the power of connection . . . with others and with ourselves.

from *A Day Late and a Dollar Short*

TERRY McMILLAN

I musta dozed off for a few minutes after they picked up my tray and the doctors checked my numbers. I know I'm in bad shape. I hate having asthma. I wasn't even born with this shit. I was forty-two when Suzie Mae called me at four-thirty in the morning to tell me that Daddy's sixteen-year-old grandson by his first wife, who he had took in, had stabbed him thirty-six times and killed him 'cause Daddy wouldn't let his girlfriend spend the night. I had a anxiety attack and couldn't catch my breath. The doctors treated me for asthma, and I been on this medication ever since. Each time I try to stop taking it, I have a attack, so my feeling is the doctors gave me this damn disease. I can't win.

And I can't lie. This attack scared me. In the back of my mind, I'm thinking: Is *this* gon' be the one? In a split second you remember everybody you love, and in the next one you ask yourself: Did I do this thing right? Did I do everything I wanted to? What would I change if I could do it all over? Did I hurt anybody so much that they won't be able to forgive me? Will they forgive me for not being perfect? I forgive myself. And I forgive God. But then you feel your eyes open and you realize you ain't dead. You got tubes coming outta you. Lights is bright. Your heart is thumping. You say a long thank-you prayer. And you lay here thinking about everything and everybody, 'cause you got another chance to live. You ask yourself what you gon' do now. My answer is plain and simple: I'ma start doing things differently, 'cause, like they say, if you keep doing what you've always done, you'll keep getting what you've always gotten. Ain't that the truth, and who don't know it?

So this is the deal, Viola. First of all, if I don't do nothing else, I'ma get this asthma under control, 'cause I'm tired of it running my life. Tired of grown kids and husbands running my life. Tired of being smart but ain't got no evidence to prove it. I wanna get my GED. I don't see why not. It ain't never too late to learn. I just hope what they say about the brain being a muscle is true. The way I see it, I figure I owe myself a cruise to *somewhere* before I hit sixty, especially since I took Paris, France, outta my dreams a million years ago. Hell, I ain't been *nowhere*. How I'ma get the money is a mystery to me, but I'll get it. If it's meant to be, it'll be. I should try to get some decent dentures: the kind that fit and don't look false. But if me or my kids ever hit the lottery, I'ma get the kind that don't come out. Paris and Janelle think playing is a waste of time and money. Paris say only emigrants and legitimate senior citizens seem to win. But Charlotte play Little Lotto three times a week, and Lewis, whenever he get a extra dollar, which ain't all that often. Both of 'em promised that if they ever hit, they would split the winnings with me. I told 'em I'd divide mine three ways if I didn't win but twenty dollars, and I would.

The first thing I would do is buy myself a house that don't need no repairs, and walk around barefoot, 'cause the carpet would be just that thick. Hell, a condo would do the trick, as long as I had a patch of dirt big enough to plant some collards, a few ears of corn, some cherry tomatoes, and hot peppers to pickle for the winter. And I'd like to know what it feel like to drive a brand-new anything. I know I'm dreaming, but deep down inside when you know your life is at least eighty percent over, you ain't got nothing left to live for but dreams.

More than anything, if something *was* to happen to me, I pray that each one of my kids find happiness. I want 'em to feel good. Live good. Do what's right. I just hope I live long enough to see Lewis get hisself together and start acting like the man I know he is. Lord knows I'd love to see Paris marry somebody worthy of her, and I'd pay cash money to be there when my grandson throw a touchdown pass on nationwide TV. And Charlotte. I hope she stop getting so mad with me for every little thing and realize that she ain't no stepchild of mine, that I love her just as much as the other kids. I want the day to come when Janelle stand on her own two feet and get rid of that rapist she married. And if I don't get my old husband back, hell, I'll settle for a new one. One thing I do know about men and kids is that they always come back. They may be a day late and a dollar short, but they always come back.

Homegirl Reunion

JOAN HOPEWELL-HARTGENS

"Say what?!" was my incredulous response to my friend Rosemary's announcement that she and a couple of other girlhood chums were planning a "homegirl reunion" for a bunch of us who had grown up together and who had already turned, or were about to turn, fifty this year.

Cynically, I thought, "They couldn't think of anything better to celebrate?" Then just as quickly, I gave thanks for how blessed I was to be alive and looking forward to my fiftieth birthday. Rosemary echoed my thoughts, "We're not making a big thing of it. Just an informal gathering of about fifteen or twenty of us who haven't seen each other in years to get together, catch up, and just celebrate our still hangin' in there." It sounded reasonable . . . possibly even enjoyable, and I had to admit I was curious . . . but!

With the exception of Rosemary and Joyce, my two best friends from back in the day, I hadn't laid eyes on most of the other girls we'd grown up with since our high school graduation thirty-three years ago, and frankly, I had been too busy in the ensuing three decades trying to make my own way in the world to have given them much thought.

"It'll be fun," my friend urged, "very relaxed—jeans and sweat suits—no stylin', I promise."

"Yeah, right!" I smiled as I recalled the frantic efforts we all used to make to outdress each other for even the most irrelevant of happenings. Then Rosemary proceeded to tick off names I hadn't heard in years.

I had left my hometown for New York City within a few months of graduating high school. My parents passed away when I was in my very early twenties, so, except for an infrequent family visit, wedding, or funeral, I had rarely gone back.

Rosemary, Joyce, and I had kept in touch over the years through phone calls, letters, and greeting cards. Periodically, more so in the past few years, the three of us had made a point of getting together at least once or twice a year, bringing each other news of our children, partners, work, triumphs, disappointments, and the occasional aches and pains. The three of us had shared secrets and aspirations since third grade, so our adult confidences seemed a natural continuation of that openness.

However, a reunion with, at this point in time, virtual strangers, struck me, who'd never even attended a high school reunion, as an altogether different and somewhat unsettling matter entirely. By the end of the conversation, I had tentatively agreed to attend, but that didn't stop me from vacillating in the weeks to come.

About a week prior to the reunion, during a telephone conversation with Joyce, who was as uncertain about attending this reunion as I was, we contemplated the wisdom of attending an affair comprised solely of menopausal women who, for the most part, we hadn't seen since we were teenagers.

In mock horror, we envisioned a roomful of middle-aged, ex-debutantes simultaneously flailing about in the throes of hot flashes and violent mood swings. For some reason, this unlikely and absurdly outdated, stereotyped scenario sent us into uncontrollable gales of giggling quite unbefitting our supposed maturity.

The night before the trip, I was once again seized by apprehension. Did I really need to see these people again? Attending would be women with whom I hadn't shared an affinity since twelfth grade. Those who for some long-forgotten reason I had resented or who, perhaps, had found displeasure with me. Others with whom I had once been close, but whose friendship had not survived beyond graduation. And only a few who, because of belonging to the same general social circle, had remained in contact.

No! I concluded. I didn't need the hassle.

But, of course, I went.

Events are rarely as portentous as one's imagination colors them. We met in a hospitality suite in one of our hometown's larger hotels, and the comfortable, casual attire that almost all of us wore camouflaged acquired bulges and flattered mature curves. Our initial, somewhat awkward, cordiality soon gave way to re-membered enjoyment as we recognized half-forgotten faces and moved just as quickly to raucous reminiscing as we acknowledged our common beginnings in a more sheltered and less complex time.

We devoured the submarine sandwiches that had been the mainstay of our adolescence as we danced to the late fifties and early sixties music of our youth and talked of friends no longer with us or lost to the exigencies of time.

Boys whose names we could barely remember, but who had rocked our worlds thirty-odd years ago, were resurrected. We spoke of dances at which we had gotten sick on cheap red wine. Recalled sweaty, dimly lit parties where we had slow dragged intently with boys sporting "processes" and stingy-brimmed hats cocked pre-cariously to the side. Remembered Friday night sorority meetings where we were given to discussing in great detail and even greater length the endless arrangements for some impending social func-tion or other. And finally, we regaled each other with raunchy tales of the clandestine goings-on after our Cotillion Ball, the event that, along with our graduation, had culminated that phase of our lives and afforded our unsuspecting parents long, satisfied sighs of relief.

Mellowed, we spoke reflectively of our lives in the intervening years. Most of us had married, and more than a few had divorced at least once. Many had relationships and children, which brought varying degrees of happiness and tribulation. Quite a few had grandchildren. Several had experienced ill health; others, harsh disappointments; and a few, devastating losses. Nearly all had jobs, some that afforded a measure of fulfillment and some that were necessary and, therefore, endured.

One woman, somewhat self-absorbed in her youth, was now an executive with a large corporation and used her position to encourage and advise young sisters just beginning their corporate climb.

Another, sober and aloof in high school, arose from her battle with a life-threatening illness to become an ardent spokesperson-activist in the fight against that disease.

A down-to-earth sister, who after working for years at the telephone company while raising a family, had just realized her dream of starting a small catering business.

Still another woman, who had gained local political prominence, remained feisty and unbowed in the aftermath of a series of bruising setbacks, ready to do battle again.

And Rosemary, who after twenty-five years of nurturing young minds as a beloved elementary school teacher, was looking forward to an early retirement and perhaps a move south to explore new horizons.

Unlike movie-of-the-week-style reunions, there were no recriminations or traumatic confrontations for decades-old real or imagined slights and deceptions. Nor were there tearful rapprochements or self-serving soul bearing. We understood the limitations of a reunion, shared only what we felt comfortable sharing, and no tender boundaries were violated.

Sisters who had been confrontational as girls had been gentled by the years. Others, who had been unassuming in their youth, had developed spirit. And those who had been considered "sadditty" had long since shed their pretentious veneers and floated down to earth.

Conversations, overlapping in that way that women's conversations do when the participants are united in support and common experience, were punctuated by exclamations of approval, encouraging smiles, empathic nods, and laughter born of the understanding that we had shared many of the same struggles.

And once again I was struck by the transforming power in the rich, full-throated laughter of Black women. That fierce, unrestrained determination to wrest joy from adversity and to savor its tart, hard-won sweetness as it trickles slowly down to the last delectable, satisfying chuckle.

We spoke of our dreams and plans for the future as enthusiastically, but certainly more selectively, than we had as girls, and jokingly reminded ourselves that in our teens the idea of even envisioning a "future" at fifty would have seemed ludicrous indeed.

As the evening wore on and we took measure of ourselves, we realized that while as yet none of us had become a household name, and although we had all made mistakes and experienced our share of heartache along the way, there was an overall sense of satisfaction with the lives we had constructed for ourselves.

Separately, yet somehow collectively, we had negotiated the past thirty-three years with a strength honed and tempered by time and nurtured while becoming young women in each other's eyes so long ago. A strength that continued to sustain us now in the fullness of our gloriously seasoned womanhood as we bopped and slopped, strolled and walked, mashed potatoed, merengued, and eventually, inevitably, we electrically slid to the end of our evening.

Before vanishing into our disparate lives, we spoke of getting together again at a future date, but, I suspect, with life being what it is, we all knew that the likelihood of that happening was tenuous at best. Yet, right then, I knew why I had come. Why we all had come. For the eighteen of us present, this coming together was much more than a reunion of "homegirls." It was a vibrant affirmation of life, growth, and the ties that bind.

Letting Go with Love

MIRIAM DeCOSTA-WILLIS

Birth and death, the violent
rhythms of the passage into and
out of life.

Mine was a childhood shrouded with images of death: uncles, dark
and gaunt, diminished by disease; aunts, silent and somber, in
mourning black; women, coming and going, in whispers; bats and
dead birds littering Charleston streets after a raging hurricane. I
learned early that loss and pain and death are a part of the fabric of
a richly textured life and that pain can sometimes underscore and
intensify a deep and loving relationship.

I have two vivid images of my last years with A. (My husband's
name was Archie Walter Willis, Jr., but people called him "A. W.,"
while family members and close friends knew him as "A.")

May 1987. We are lying on the beach at Pointe du Bout, where
clouds move imperceptibly across a sky that changes from pink
to deep purple. I frame mental pictures, intent on remembering:
palm trees etched against a darkening sky, sailboats anchored off
shore, and seagulls in the distance. I hold this minute tight. We
touch, but are lost in separate thoughts: memories of the day—the
slave cabins at Leyritz Plantation and the rain forest resplendent
with hibiscus and anthuriums—and anticipation of the night,
when we will make love as if for the last time.

Later that year, I am driving home through Memphis streets after a long faculty meeting. It is already dark and the deserted streets
are wet from a late-fall rainstorm. I am cold and exhausted after a
long and difficult day, when . . . my thoughts turn to A, home alone,
waiting for me, sitting in the little room off our bedroom. I feel as

though I am traveling through a long, dark tunnel at the end of which stands my husband, encircled by a warm, golden light. Transfigured, I move toward his light.

Joy in the midst of pain, for November was the beginning of the end. We recognized the signs—increased discomfort, weight loss, hoarseness, disorientation, and slurred speech—and we knew that the dark spots on the bone scan indicated that cancer had metastasized throughout his body. I held back tears when the doctor advised, "I would strongly urge you to get your affairs in order, Mr. Willis, because things might get quite difficult by the end of the year."

Actually, it had been a difficult two years. The discovery in August 1985 of a dark spot on the chest X-ray, surgery two weeks later, and a one-month recuperation at home, followed by a long hiatus of apparent remission. But always, always was the uncertainty, the urgency to seize life, the feeling that every minute should be savored, relished. And then, in the spring of 1987, we learned that A's condition was terminal, that there were clusters of ring-shaped malignant tumors on both sides of his brain. That spring we prepared for his illness.

Now we had to get ready for his dying.

I say "we" because we confronted his illness and death together. I did the research: read books on cancer; ordered inspirational tapes; talked to doctors, pharmacists, and nutritionists; and called hospitals, cancer centers, and hotlines throughout the country. After I collected the data, we made decisions about treatment and care; we agreed, for example, that he would be cared for at home and that he would die at home. We also decided to be open and honest about his condition; too often, in Memphis at least, cancer patients and their families hide behind a veil of secrecy that requires so much emotional and psychic energy to maintain. It was very helpful for A to be able to talk about his illness. Openness and knowledge about the disease gave us a feeling, however tenuous, of control.

Our take-charge attitude sometimes had humorous consequences. When a battery of doctors visited A the day of his release from the hospital, we handed them a list of detailed questions that I had prepared. The first question read: "How soon can we have sex?" When the doctors responded with an embarrassed silence, we concluded that they could prevent dying but didn't understand much about "living." A month later, I turned to the oncologist after A's first bout with chemotherapy and asked, "What about sex?" The doctor mumbled, "Uh, maybe after six months. Er, sometimes it takes a year." He would be dismayed to know that we went right home and fell into each other's arms.

Although there were often passionless days and impotent nights, physical intimacy between us was very important because it affirmed who we were as individuals and how we connected as lovers. It reminded us that we were *alive.* Our lovemaking was an important ritual in the pattern of our lives; a quiet dinner, wine, bubblebath, candlelight, soft music, and gentle caresses were a prelude to a deeply satisfying physical communication. I was aware, however, of subtle changes in my feelings. After his surgery, I was more subdued, less enthusiastic about sex because I was afraid of hurting him, of pressing against the deep, painful scar that encircled his chest and back. And sometimes, in those last few months, when I held him in my arms and felt his thin, frail body against me, tears ran down my cheeks.

At age fifty, a time when I was facing changes—menopause; my daughters' marriages, divorces, and childbirths; and stressful problems at work—I had to deal with the illness and death of a man whom I loved deeply. Both of us had been married before, and so we brought to this second marriage of thirteen years all the ten-

derness, sensitivity, and understanding of a mature and responsible love. I think that A, a very sensitive and compassionate man,
worried most about me when he became ill, and tried valiantly to
prepare me, emotionally and financially, for life without him. An
attorney, he had founded a mortgage company and was actively
involved in downtown development, property renovation, and
low-income housing, but had spread himself too thin and had
problems: tax bills, mounting debts, and an inadequate cash flow.
He struggled desperately to keep the business going, while shor-
ing up resources to support us during a protracted illness. We put
everything on the table: our expenses, debts, wills, bank accounts
and property deeds. There were no hidden agendas, because we
were in this thing together. I tried to assure him that I could support us, although my teaching position at a small, private, histori-
cally Black college did not pay much. "We can always sell the
house and your car," I told him, concerned that worry would ex-
acerbate his already precarious health. I wonder sometimes, in retrospect, how on earth two married people can manage in a crisis
without honesty and trust.

During his illness, we achieved an emotional intimacy that was
more intense, more fulfilling, than any physical pleasure that we
had ever experienced, primarily because A was so open and caring.
I remember, particularly, the evenings we spent taping questions
and answers about his work as a civil rights attorney, state legisla-
tor, and mortgage banker for the biography that I will write. There
was a special magic in those hours we shared: A seated to my left in
pajamas and bathrobe, his voice low and hoarse, recalling the people and events of his past; me scribbling notes in my pad while the
tape recorder hummed between us.

We tried, even after that dark November, to live as normal a life
as possible in spite of frequent visits to doctors and hospitals for

tests, radiation treatment, and chemotherapy. I had to take him to work and friends would bring him home, because he was unable to drive. As late as February of 1988—five months before his death—A flew to Nashville to lobby for the Lorraine Civil Rights Museum and to attend a meeting of the Tennessee Racing Commission, community service for which he received no compensation. His determination to work in the face of fatigue, depression, constant pain and severe weight loss (he weighed only 124 pounds by that time) was a lesson in living and dying with grace and dignity. Imperceptibly, however, the pace of our lives began to change, and we spent quiet days in slow motion. The two of us would sit outside on the patio for hours while he dozed in his chair and I looked out over the garden, feeling very much alone.

There were, though, moments to savor: presentation of an award to A by the governor, a testimonial banquet for him in November, the dedication of the A. W. Willis Bridge in December, Christmas dinner with our large extended family, a performance of *Peter Pan* with four of our grandchildren, and a portrait-taking session with our twenty-six-member family. Often we laughed together about the most awful things. In the oncologist's office, for example, he whispered, "Hey, Runt, looks like we landed on death row!"; and when, toward the end, we discussed his funeral plans, he chuckled, "I know you'll do it right. If not, I'll plan it my damn self." Once, we even cried together. While I was completing a paper to deliver in North Carolina the following day, A walked into my study and said, "I want to tell you good-bye," and then that strong, courageous man started crying. The idea of my leaving and the possibility of his dying alone frightened him, and he admitted, through tears, "I'm scared." (That was the only time in his long struggle with cancer that he ever expressed any fear; he told me that only two things worried him: unbearable pain and a long illness that left me in debt.) I put my arms around him, kissed him, and said, "I won't go. I'll stay here with you." Convinced that he would die that night, however, he didn't want to go to bed, so I took him in my arms and gently massaged his body. When he awoke the next morning, he said, "I made it through the night. The Lord has spared me one more time." Although I didn't have the solace of the church, A had a deep, abiding faith that sustained him through turbulent nights, when he dreamed that he couldn't wake up or witnessed his own funeral.

As the primary caregiver, I went through the same stages that A and other seriously ill people experienced: disbelief, denial, shock, fear, anger, depression, rage, and a pain so deep that at times I could not breathe or even think straight. After the meeting with the doctor in November, I wrote in my journal: "I thought I had prepared myself emotionally for every eventuality, but with each onslaught of the disease I ache and am in such pain. I feel as if someone is squeezing my chest, as if there is a heavy weight pressing me down and sapping my energy."

Pain seeped through the cracks of my carefully constructed wall, a protective wall that I built up over months of reading, for I always turned to books for solace, comfort, and escape, aware that the words of others could help me through traumatic experiences. Books like Audre Lorde's *The Cancer Journals*, Gerda Lerner's *A Death of One's Own*, and Elisabeth Kubler-Ross's *On Death and Dying* helped me understand what A was going through; relaxation tapes—with the sounds of waterfalls, rain forests, and the sea—calmed my nerves; and Louise Hay's self-healing tapes alleviated my depression. Through creative visualization, I began to rehearse my life without A, creating an imaginary future in another place with new friends and a different lifestyle.

And I tried, really tried, to take care of myself, first, because A depended on me, and second, because I needed good health to cope with his illness and, later, to make a new life without him. After learning that the illness was terminal, I joined a health-and-fitness center, and the following spring, during the really rough period, I started a diet program and lost twenty-five pounds. Eating right and exercising gave me a feeling of control in a situation that was very hard for me, a highly structured person, to deal with.

In spite of my carefully constructed defenses, there were times when I slipped over the edge. I was often tired—no, exhausted—because I got very little sleep, particularly during that last spring when A was so agitated and restless. He would get up eight or ten times during the night, turn on the lights, stumble around, and cough loudly. Sometimes, when he awakened at 2 A.M., unable to sleep because of pain or depression, I would listen while he talked about his plans for low-income housing or for the Lorraine Civil Rights Museum, but then I couldn't go back to sleep. I was depressed and tense one day, irritable and nervous the next. Frequently, I had difficulty concentrating, which was devastating for my work. That year, I designed an honors program for which I had to write grant proposals, and I taught the first interdisciplinary honors course, which included guest lectures, visits to cultural events, and trips to conferences—all of which taxed my energy and creativity. Somehow, I muddled through, fearing that I would never write again because my life force was ebbing away.

At times I was impatient or sharp with A. Once, when I was very tired and had a bad cold, I told him, "I'm so tired of talking about cancer. I just can't take it any longer. I'm doing the best I can, but I'm under a lot of stress, too." I felt so ashamed of myself, a few days later, when I heard him tell his youngest daughter how supportive I'd been, that he couldn't have made it without me. I tried so hard to hold my sharp tongue in check, but occasionally I let loose. The month before I started losing weight, he teased, "You sure are getting fat," and I shot back, "But *I'm* healthy!" That was really hitting below the belt, but I was feeling so bad about myself; I looked dumpy and matronly, and I had terrible bags under my eyes.

The hardest part was dealing with powerful contradictory impulses: attraction to a man I deeply loved, but aversion to his wasted, scarred, sickly body; desire to spend time with him, but feeling trapped; comfort in having people around, while longing for privacy and time alone; concern about his care, but fear for my future. Occasionally, I felt guilty or ashamed of those very human feelings, but I was doing the best that I could to care for and nurture my husband, while trying to hold on to my own sanity. My journal was an important tool in struggling with anxiety, ambivalence, and contradictory feelings. Sometimes it was hard to confront the ugly part of me. I thought how much easier it is, so much less painful, to stand at the periphery of life — to avoid too much intimacy with others, to treat the surface realities, and to eschew deep reflection on darker feelings: shame, guilt, anger, and self-loathing. Three months before A's death, I wrote in my journal: "All day I was tense and numb, the result no doubt of depression. I felt a little like I did last April — tired, removed from everything, despondent. I felt as if the walls were closing in on me. I didn't want to come home; I just wanted to run away."

No, I didn't run away, but I did, on occasion, escape, physically and psychologically. I would slip off from work in the afternoon to view a foreign film or, if friends came to visit A, head for the park with a book, blanket, and sandwich in hand. Lying under dogwood trees beside the lake, I found the peace and serenity that could take me through another week. One of my coping mechanisms is to withdraw into myself, my work, my own interests, and so when things got rough, I found myself starting to distance myself psychologically from my husband and his illness.

Those last few months were an emotional roller coaster ride because A began to have mood swings, which the doctor had warned us about; he became delusional and, once or twice, hostile. When he was no longer able to go to the office, he began to do things around the house because he needed to feel like a functioning human being; he would dig up the flowers, chop up garbage to cook, and leave the broiler on all day. I couldn't leave him alone after that. One night, I woke up to find him standing over me in the dark, asking where his guns were because he had to shoot someone. Another night, he walked up to the bed and said, "I'm going to take you with me." I jumped up and screamed, "The hell you are!" I have to smile about those incidents now, but they were very unsettling at the time. I often had to remind myself that cancer, particularly brain tumors, had changed the man I loved. After an especially difficult day, when I crawled into bed, he accused me of not caring about him, of being wrapped up in myself, of caring more about my women friends. Later, he turned to my son and said very calmly, "Your mother's a lesbian," probably because he overheard me laughing and talking with friends—my primary outlet during that period of confinement. The next day, I wrote in my journal, "He looked at me last night with such hatred. Where did the love go?"

That brief phase was followed by a period of tremendous anxiety and dependence on me; he fretted when I left home, called frequently, and summoned me out of classes and meetings. Although I had a woman to stay with him while I was in class, I took care of him when I came home: bathed, shaved, and dressed him; massaged him with lotion; watched movies with him at night. In early June, when I tried to help him up out of his chair, he collapsed to the floor, and I had to leave him there, resting on a pillow and covered with a blanket, until morning, when I called our son-in-law to help me get him up. When his condition worsened and he became completely bedridden, I hired nurses. The doctor offered to hospitalize him after the situation became difficult for me, but I think that hospitals too often function like nursing homes — warehousing the sick and shielding the family from the harsher realities of sickness and dying. I wanted to keep A at home, where he and I could share his last days, the children and grandchildren could visit him, and he could die peacefully, surrounded by loved ones.

But the world was too much with me those last weeks: nurses on eight-hour shifts, nine grown children (his and mine) chatting until late at night, kids running through the house, and daughters sprawled across our bed. Most days, we had several visitors, but one Sunday I counted twenty-six people, some playing basketball outside, others lounging around the pool, still others opening the refrigerator, and even a few invading my private space — my study. That was the place where I went to cry *alone,* because I had been taught by my stoic parents to suffer in silence, never complaining or feeling sorry for myself. Now I didn't even have a place for my private pain.

Eventually, I converted our bedroom into a sickroom: set up a hospital bed, ordered an oxygen tank, bought medical supplies, replaced the perfume bottles on my dresser with codeine tablets and liquid morphine. Twice, I took him to the hospital for blood transfusions, while my stepdaughter and I sat with him, talking, reading, and writing letters. Their father's illness created a close bond between me and A's five children by a previous marriage, and I called them often for advice, help, and support.

One afternoon in mid-July, while my sister-in-law and I were talking in my study, the nurse came down the hall and said, "I think Mr. Willis has gone." I walked into our room, bent down, and whispered in his ear, "I love you. I'll miss you."

I used to tell my best friend, "I'm so lucky," but she would smile and say, "No, you're blessed." Indeed, I have been truly blessed to have known and loved a man like A, to have shared a life with him, and to have accompanied him on his final rite of passage. Those last three years were a gift.

Now, when I close my eyes and images of uncles and widowed aunts flicker before me — men who died and women who cared for them — I understand the meaning of love and the profound connection between life and death.

from *The Women of Brewster Place*

GLORIA NAYLOR

Mattie got up Sunday morning to the usual banging and howling in the house on weekends. Miss Eva was in the kitchen fighting with the children.

"Grandma, Basil broke my crayon. See, he bit it right in half—and on purpose!" Lucielia wailed.

"Basil, you little red devil, come here! Can't I cook breakfast in peace?"

"But, Miss Eva, Ciel took my coloring book and she tore all the pages."

"I did not," Ciel protested, and kicked him.

Basil began crying.

"Why, you evil, narrow-tailed heifer. I'll break your neck!" And she smacked Ciel on the behind with her wooden cooking spoon.

Basil stopped crying instantly in order to enjoy Ciel's punishment. "Goody, goody." He stuck out his tongue at her.

"Goody, goody, on you, Mister," Miss Eva went after him with the spoon, "I ain't forgot you broke my china poodle this morning."

Basil ducked under the table, knowing she wouldn't be able to bend and reach him.

"Want me to get him for you, Grandma?" Ciel offered, trying to get back into her good graces.

"No, I just want you both out of my kitchen. Out! Out!" She banged the table with the spoon.

Mattie stood yawning in the kitchen door. "Can't there be just one morning of peace and quiet in this house—just one?" Ciel and Basil both ran to her, each trying to outshout the other about their various injustices. "I don't want to hear it," Mattie sighed. "It's too early for this nonsense. Now go wash up for breakfast—you're still in pajamas."

"Didn't you hear her? Now, get!" Miss Eva shouted and raised her spoon.

The children ran upstairs. Eva smiled behind their backs and turned toward the stove.

"Well, good morning," Mattie said, and poured herself a cup of coffee.

" 'Tain't natural, just 'tain't natural," Miss Eva grumbled at the stove.

"They're only children, Miss Eva. All children are like that."

"I ain't talking about them children, I'm talking 'bout you. You done spent another weekend holed up in this house and ain't gone out nowhere."

"Now that's not true. Friday night I went to choir practice, and Saturday I took Basil to get a pair of shoes and then a double feature at the Century, which is why I overslept this morning. That only leaves Sunday morning, Miss Eva, and there's church today, and then I gotta go back to work tomorrow. So I don't know what you're talkin' about."

"What I'm talkin' 'bout is that I ain't heard you mention no man involved in all them exciting goings-on in your life—church and children and work. It ain't natural for a young woman like you to live that way. I can't remember the last time no man come by to take you out."

Mattie couldn't remember either. There had been a bus ride with a foreman in the shipping department at her job and she had gone out a few times with one of the ushers in her church—but that was last spring, or was it last winter?

"Humph," Mattie shrugged her shoulders and sipped her coffee. "I've been so busy, I guess I haven't noticed. It has been a long time, but so what? I've got my hands full raising my son."

"Children get raised overnight, Mattie. Then what you got? I should know. I raised seven and four of my grand and they all gone except Ciel. But I'm an old woman, my life's most over. That ain't no excuse for you. Why, by the time I was your age, I was on my second husband, and you still slow about gettin' the first."

"Well, Miss Eva, I'd have to had started twenty years ago to beat your record," Mattie kidded.

"I ain't making no joke, child." And her watery eyes clouded over as she stared at the younger woman. Mattie knew that look well. The old woman wanted a confrontation and would not be budged. "Ain't you ever had no needs in that direction? No young woman wants an empty bed, year in and year out."

Mattie felt the blood rushing to her face under Miss Eva's open stare. She took a few sips of coffee to give herself time to think. Why didn't she ever feel that way? Was there really something wrong with her? The answers were beyond her at that moment, but Miss Eva was waiting, and she had to say something.

"My bed hasn't been empty since Basil was born," she said lightly, "and I don't think anyone but me would put up with the way that boy kicks in his sleep."

As soon as the words were out, she regretted them. This was an ancient battle between the two women.

"Basil needs a bed of his own. I been telling you that for years."

"He's afraid of the dark. You know that."

"Most children are afraid at first, but they get used to it."

"I'm not gonna have my child screaming his head off all night just to please you. He's still a baby, he doesn't like sleeping alone, and that's it!" she said through clenched teeth.

"Five years old ain't no baby," Miss Eva said. And then she added mildly, "You sure it's Basil who don't want to sleep alone?"

The gentle pity in the faded blue eyes robbed Mattie of the angry accusations she wanted to fling at the old woman for making her feel ashamed. Shame for what? For loving her son, wanting to protect him from his invisible phantoms that lay crouching in the dark? No, those pitying eyes had slid into her unconscious like a blue laser and exposed secrets that Mattie had buried from her own self. They had crept between her sheets and knew that her body had hungered at moments, had felt the need for a filling and caressing of inner spaces. But in those restless moments she had turned toward her manchild and let the soft, sleeping flesh and the thought of all that he was and would be draw those yearnings onto the edge of her lips and the tips of her fingers. And she could not sleep until she released those congested feelings by stroking his moist forehead and planting a kiss there. A mother's kiss for a sleeping child. And this old woman's freakish blue eyes had turned it into something to make her ashamed.

She wanted to get up from the table and spit into those eyes, beat them sightless—those that had befriended her, kept her baby from sharp objects and steep stairs while she worked, wept with her over the death of her parents—she wanted them crushed under her fists for daring to make her ashamed of loving her son.

"I don't have to take this," Mattie stammered defensively. "Just because we stay in your house don't give you a right to tell me how to raise my child. I'm a boarder here, or at least I would be if you'd let me pay you. Just tell me how much I owe you, and I'll pay up and be out before the week's over."

"I ain't decided yet."

"You been saying that for five years!" Mattie was frustrated.

"And you been movin' every time I mention anything about that little spoiled nigger of yours. You still saving my rent money in the bank, ain't you?"

"Of course." Mattie had religiously put aside money every month, and her account had grown quite large.

"Good, you'll be using it soon enough for new clothes for my funeral. That is, if you plan on coming?"

Mattie looked at Miss Eva's stooped back and the wrinkled yellow neck with grizzled wisps of hair lying on it, and small needles of repentance began to stab at her heart. She would be gone soon, and Mattie didn't want to imagine facing the loss of another mother.

"You're a crafty old woman. You always try to win an argument by talkin' about some funeral. You're too ornery to die, and you know it."

Miss Eva chuckled. "Some folks do say that. To tell you the truth, I had planned on stayin' till I'm a hundred."

Please do, Mattie thought sadly, and then said aloud, "No, I couldn't bear you that long—maybe till ninety-nine and a half."

They smiled at each other and silently agreed to put the argument to rest.

The children came running into the kitchen, scrubbed and penitent. "Let me check those ears," Mattie said to Ciel and Basil.

She was about to send him back upstairs to wash his when he put his arms around her neck and said, "Mama, I forgot to kiss you hello this morning." Basil knew he would win his reprieve this way. Miss Eva knew it, too, but she said nothing as she slung the oatmeal into the bowls and slowly shook her head.

Mattie was aware of only the joy that these unsolicited acts of tenderness gave her. She watched him eating his oatmeal, intent on each mouthful that he swallowed because it was keeping her son alive. It was moving through his blood and creating skin cells and hair cells and new muscles that would eventually uncurl and multiply and stretch the skin on his upper arms and thighs, elongate the plump legs that only reached the top rung of his chair. And when they had reached the second rung, Miss Eva would be dead.

Her children would have descended upon the beautiful house and stripped it of all that was valuable and sold the rest to Mattie. Her parents would have carried away a screaming Ciel, and as Mattie would look around the gutted house, she'd know why the old yellow woman had made her save her money. She had wanted her spirit to remain in this house through the memory of someone who was capable of loving it as she had. While Basil's legs pushed down toward the third rung, Mattie would be working two jobs to carry the mortgage on the house. Her son must have room to grow in, a yard to run in, a decent place to bring his friends. Her own spirit must one day have a place to rest because the body could not, as it pushed and struggled to make all around them safe and comfortable. It would all be for him and those to come from the long, muscular thighs of him who sat opposite her at the table.

Mattie looked at the man who was gulping coffee and shoveling oatmeal into his mouth. "Why you eating so fast? You'll choke."

"I got some place to go."

"It's Sunday, Basil. You been runnin' all weekend. I thought you were gonna stay home and help me with the yard."

"Look, I'm only going out for a few minutes. I told you I'll cut the grass, and I will, so stop hassling me."

Mattie remained silent because she didn't want to argue with him while he ate. He'd had a nervous stomach all his life, and she didn't want him to get cramps or run out of the house, refusing to eat at all. She doubted that she would see him anymore that day, and she wanted to be certain he got at least one decent meal.

"All right, you want more toast or coffee?" she offered, as way of apology.

He really didn't, but he let her fix him another cup to show that he was no longer annoyed. He thanked her by remaining to finish his breakfast.

"Okay, I'll see you in a while," he said, and pushed his chair back. "Hey, could you lend me a coupla dollars to get some gas for the car?" He saw that she had opened her mouth to refuse and went on, "I don't want it for today but tomorrow, I gotta go looking for another job. I don't pick up my check from the last place until Thursday, and I don't wanna waste four days sitting around here doing nothing." He bent down and whispered in her ear, "You know I'm not the kind of guy to hang around and let a woman support him." Seeing her smile, he straightened up and said, "But I would make a good pimp, wouldn't I, Mama?" And he panto-mimed putting on a cocked hat and strutted in the middle of the floor.

Mattie laughed and openly scorned his foolish antics while in-wardly admitting that he had to be considered attractive by many women. Basil looked exactly like his father, but the clean, natu-rally curved lines of Butch's mouth seemed transformed into a mild sullenness when placed on Basil's face. His clear brown eyes were heavily lashed, and many young women had discovered just one heartbeat too late that his slightly drooping eyelids were not mirrors of boyish seductiveness but hardened apathy.

Mattie had never met any of Basil's girlfriends, and he rarely mentioned them. She thought about this as she gave him the money and watched him leave the house. She cleared off the breakfast dishes, and it suddenly came to her that she hadn't met many of his male friends either. Where was he going? She truly didn't know, and it had come to be understood that she was not to ask. How long had it been that way? Surely, it had happened within moments. It seemed that only hours ago he had been the child who could hug her neck and talk himself out of a spanking, who had brought home crayoned valentines, and had cried when she went to her second job. So then, who was this stranger who had done away with her little boy and left her with no one and so alone?

Mattie pondered this as her hands plunged into the soapy dishwater, and she mechanically washed bowls and silverware. She tried to recapture the years and hold them up for inspection, so she could pinpoint the transformation, but they slipped through her fingers and slid down the dishes, hidden under the iridescent bubbles that broke with the slightest movement of her hand. She quickly saw that it was an impossible task and abandoned the effort. He had grown up, that was all. She looked up from the sink and gasped as she caught her reflection in the windowpane — but when had she grown old?

Any possible answer had disappeared down the drain with the used dishwater, and she watched it go without regret and scoured the porcelain until it shone. She changed the freshly starched kitchen curtains and rewaxed the tiles. She went through the house vacuuming clean carpets and dusting spotless tables — these were the testimony to her lost years. There was a need to touch and smell and see that it was all in place. It would always be there to comfort and affirm when she would have nothing else.

She could not find the little boy whom this had all been for, but she found an old cut-glass bowl that she washed and polished and filled with autumn flowers from her yard. She put the bowl on a windowsill in her sun porch, and, exhausted, sat among the huge vines and plants, watching the fading sun dissolve into the prismed edges of the bowl. She loved this room above all the others — a place to see things grow. And she had watched and coaxed and nurtured the greenery about her. Miss Eva's presence was there in the few pieces of china bric-a-brac that Mattie had saved over the years. And it was here that she would come and sit when there was a problem or some complex decision to be made. She felt guilty about missing church that day, but if God were everywhere, surely He was here among so much natural beauty and peace. So Mattie sat there and prayed, but sometimes her supplications for comfort were to the wisdom of a yellow, blue-eyed spirit who had foreseen this day and had tried to warn her.

Mattie sat there for hours, and still Basil did not come. She looked at the long grass and decided to cut it the next day after work, if her back didn't bother her too much. It was becoming more difficult each year to keep up the house alone. She got up from the couch stiffly and climbed the steps toward her bedroom.

Her house slippers scraped the edges of the steps. Irresponsible, his counselors had said in school. High-natured, she had replied in her heart. Hadn't he said that they were always picking on him; everyone had been against him, except her. She had been the refuge when he ran from school to school, job to job. They wanted too much. She had been so proud that he always turned to her— fled to her when he accused them of demanding the impossible. "Irresponsible"—the word whispered on the soft carpet as her feet dragged up the dark stairs. She had demanded nothing all these years, never doubting that he would be there when needed. She had carefully pruned his spirit to rest only in the enclaves of her will, and she had willed so little that he had been tempted to return again and again over the last thirty years because his just being had been enough to satisfy her needs. But now her back was tightening in the mornings, and her grass was growing wild and ragged over the walkway while she pulled herself painfully up the stairs alone.

BABIES??!!

TINA McELROY ANSA

*He maketh the barren woman to keep house and to be a joyful
mother of spiritual children. Praise ye the Lord.*

— Psalm 113:9

Like so many women who came of age in the sixties and seventies
of the last century, I not only thought I could have it all—family,
career, travel, interesting life—I thought I had all the time in the
world to have it. I didn't. None of us does.

So, at age forty-four or so, I looked up to discover that menopause was looming, and I was still childless. Married, happy, working away at my third novel, but childless.

Oh, my, I thought, I better do something about this! But in the
next two years or so, I did not become pregnant. Which suited
my husband—the father of a beautiful, vibrant twenty-something
baby girl—the baby daddy baby, for real—just fine. And I wasn't
that upset either. Until . . .

Until my gynecologist and I had a talk, and he informed me
that the fibroids growing in my uterus were becoming so large, they
were posing a health risk. I needed to make a decision about surgery. That's when I changed Ob-Gyns, to Dr. Sharon, a Spelman
College sister. However, laser surgery did not work. Neither did
changing my diet nor filling my womb with love. She said the same
thing.

Everything changed.

I got rid of my IUD. I tried quickly to get pregnant. I waited
a couple of years to have the surgery. It did not happen. While I
waited, I questioned my sanity.

Was I nuts? Was I crazy? How could I have waited so long (until my forties) to begin seriously to try? How could I have been so content for so long without a child in my life, without MY child in my life? What had I done, Lord? What made me think I still had all the time in the world when time was ticking by so swiftly?

I would get up in the night and go to the bathroom to cry and moan privately, in solitude, where I could cry out to God and ask, "Why? Why did you let me make this horrendous and prodigious mistake with my life? Here I am with so much to pass on to my child."

One night He answered me. "Tina?" He called, real puzzlement in His voice. "What are you crying about?"

"Oh, God, you know," I sobbed. "I waited too long to have a baby. I didn't have a baby in my twenties or in my thirties; and now here I am in my forties and I am going to have a hysterectomy. Now it's too late, and I can't seem to have a baby now and everything."

I sobbed some more before He answered, still with confusion in His voice. "Babies?! You crying about *babies?!*"

"Un-huh," I sniffled, wiping my face with a wadded-up piece of tear-soaked toilet tissue.

"Shoot," He said, almost sucking His teeth at me. "Babies? I send babies to the world every instant. And you're sitting there on the bathroom floor crying about *babies?!*"

Even in my misery, His voice and what He said resonated with me. But as my mother says, "You can show a Negro quicker than you can tell 'em." God proceeded to show me.

Before I had time to have my surgery or to consider seriously adoption, the universe began sending me babies.

Afrika, my husband's baby, who informed me after one too many references to her as my stepdaughter, " 'Stepdaughter?,' that doesn't really sound right, does it? It doesn't sound like what I am to you. Why don't you just call me your daughter." Then, my friend Blanchie made me official "co-grandmother" of her little ones.

Then, my good friend Georgene became pregnant, and I was honored with being Zora-Bug's godmother and chose the title "Nana Tina." I mean the babies just kept on coming. "I love you, Aunt Tina," I came home to hear on the answering machine. Each night when my writer friend Dawn read the alphabet book to her daughter Hannah, " 'T' is for Tina," they said together.

It seemed right after that conversation in the bathroom, God was sending babies to ME in every instant.

Play babies, godbabies, grandbabies, nieces, nephews, great-nieces, grand-nephews, my daughter's cousin's babies.

I truly had to holler, "Okay, okay, okay, God! I get it, I get it! Hold up on the babies, I'm running out of space!!"

We achieving childless black women have a real role to play in the shaping of our world, in the lives of the children God sends to the world. It is no small thing to be "Auntie Tina," "Aunt Tina," "Nana Tina," "My Tina," "Grandma Tina," "Not the Mama Tina." Just stop and think of the women who played those roles in our lives when we were girls.

God let up for a little while with the babies sent to me, just long enough for me to catch my breath.

Then, just in case I forgot, He recently started again.

"Hello, Auntie Tina," was the message on my machine a couple of weeks ago from my friend Sheryl Lee's youngest. "This is Coco. Thank you for the cards you sent to me and [my brother] Etienne. I love you. Bye-bye."

BABIES?? Shoot, God sends babies to the world every instant.

Adoption: A Midlife Love Story

SHEILA STAINBACK

"I can see I'm going to have start putting away money for that child's psychiatrist in the future." That was the first reaction of a friend of twenty years when I sat across from him nearly a year ago telling him I had decided to adopt a child, specifically a black boy under age three. I had kept this plan to myself for years, fearing just that kind of pointed and ultimately hurtful remark. As a hard-driven TV journalist who also spent her free time working as an officer of the National Association of Black Journalists, I had never struck anyone who knew me well as a person who would make time for a child. I learned from close associates that my nickname was "ice queen."

I have long felt overwhelmed by this desire to do something for children in need. I have given thousands of dollars to child advocacy programs and joined the board of a foster agency, all in an effort to do more than just cover the latest story of child abuse. I also tried to avoid such stories because they left me feeling so helpless and overwhelmed with grief. I wasn't conscious of a ticking biological clock—indeed, the idea of giving birth held little or no appeal for me. Still, children stayed stubbornly on my middle-aged mind for the last ten years. "Listen to your passions," one friend advised, and I gave more money.

Then it hit me, just before my forty-plus birthday: I didn't necessarily want to give birth—I wanted to be a mother. But having children represented instant poverty to me because the folks I knew who were parents complained constantly about money, especially about not having enough. My focus had been on building my 401(k), and the thought of saving for a college education for a child was beyond me. I'd have to work full-time at least until I was eighty! And I truly loved my life of seeing a movie anytime I wanted; dining with friends at the latest "hot" New York restaurant; buying a new wardrobe of clothes for every season; and most of all—sleeping late every weekend. How would I merge this single-ton thinking with being a mom? Eventually, the decision for me was so easy, I can see why it shocked even my closest friends.

I simply decided that I didn't want the second half of my life to look like the first. Like every news story I tackled, I set out to find a way to bring a child into my life before another year had passed and to hell with sleep and fine clothes.

I signed up for foster/adoptive parent classes at Brooklyn's Angel Guardian agency, June 1, 2001, amassing thirty hours in train-ing on what it means to bring a child who is not biologically yours into your home. Most of the people who took these courses were other black women trying to become foster parents; almost all the white folks in attendance wanted to adopt; I was the only black per-son in attendance who wanted to adopt a child.

I first got to know my son Charles just six weeks after I was certified to be a foster/adoptive parent, by opening his picture that had been sent to me via e-mail exactly a week after the September 11 attacks. While weary New Yorkers and the nation feared for what might happen next, feeling forever changed, I was focused on meeting this new young man who would forever change me. Charles has huge, expressive eyes, a megawatt smile; and thick curly hair that's never been cut and has been braided in cornrows since he was a year old.

He called me "mommy" for the first time just five days after he moved in on November 7, 2001. Charles was born to a drug-addicted mother, though he had no drugs in his system at birth. My little Pisces is bright, beautiful, and full of life. His foster mother took him in when he was two weeks old after his birth mother left him in the hospital. Charles landed in my life (and luckily for me) because his foster mother at age sixty-three felt she would not have the energy to raise him.

Now, my spacious one-bedroom apartment, cleared of journalistic clippings and clutter weeks before his arrival, is awash with orange trucks, dozens of race cars, and every item connected to the *Blues Clues* franchise. I've exchanged my silks and high heels for washable cotton and cross-training shoes; the only fine dining I do is at Mickey D's every other week; and the next movie I see will likely be G-rated and on a Saturday afternoon with scores of other moms and kids.

I love my life more than ever. While I've always been proud of my Emmy award, being a leader in several journalists groups, and getting to know some of the most famous and powerful people in the world, none of it compares to my son's smile and hugs. And bath rituals. And bedtime stories. And watching him learn how to dress and undress himself. Ahead lie potty training, braces, and report cards. At a time when my peers will be bouncing their grandchildren on their knees, I'll be helping Charles select a tuxedo for a prom. I wouldn't trade that future and my life for anything else in the world.

The Pathway Home

STEPHANIE ROSE BIRD

Ambling down the path, boxes and bags held snug, when the vision of a new home in the distance offsets my balance, causing a pause. A cursory glance over the barren gray dirt that someone thought was a yard, and a plan hatches: a couple of forsythia bushes over there, a smattering of deep purple Dutch iris here, maybe some double-blooming raspberry-scented pink peonies right there, a cluster of sweetly fragrant lilies closest to the front door, would be a nice touch. Yes! At long last—a creative plan to fill the void.

We waddle back and forth—arms brimming with precious possessions. Just before dusk with the boxes, bags, paintings, sculptures, and tatty furniture tucked safely indoors, it is time to venture back outside. After living in the inner city with barely a tree over five years old, having a yard, however barren and small, is an emancipation.

What would Mama think? There is none of the bucolic splendor here that I was accustomed to as a child. This tight and tidy brick two-flat is only a stone's throw away from the El tracks. Once the view from my bedroom window was of a verdant lake rimmed with sweeping pines and sleepy willows. Now I look out over the canyon created by the expressway and a river of ever-flowing, noisy vehicles. At this point in my life, I realize the world is as beautiful as my imagination permits.

I plow the soil diligently with my hand tools, flipping her over and over again with my pitchfork. Soon enough it becomes evident that, like me, she is still very fertile. As I dig down deep, I find the soil to be as rich and black as a Yoruban queen. Within these dark depths, I plant an array of seeds and bulbs: lullabies at night for the little one; sunny daffodils by day to light the way for the boys; purple *Viola wittrockiana,* Mama's color in her memory; hope for the healthy birth of the little girl growing within my still-flat belly; *Hyacinthus hybrid,* narcissus, and *Tulipa greigii* for my grandmas; Negro spirituals, a tribute to Grandpop; shiny pennies are tossed for luck; *Achillea filipendulina* for Great-grandma Louise; sensual Bourbonnais roses for my dear aunt Rose; daily water and fire rituals for clarity, strength, and protection; *Aquilegia vulgaris* for my second "Mum" Iris who radiates gentility, power, and grace; rites of fertility, recipes for continued health, creativity, and the infinite capacity to love; anchored by a round cairn of stone symbolic of my soul mate, all set behind a white-washed picket fence that seemed to begin aging as soon as it was erected (sprinkled with gopher's dust to bar evil spirits from entry), . . . and so it went for over a decade.

Now it's time to venture out to the local market for groceries. It is the dawn of the new millennium. A beautiful late-spring afternoon. I sit on the front stoop, woozy from the scent of lilac in high season. Time to make a shopping list for supper. My husband has been wearing down. He looks tired, but in the morning he requests tacos. I nod and agree that it is most definitely a good day for "Mexican," all the while hoping inside that this spicy meal might revive his energy by warming his soul. I draft a shopping list:

3 pounds of plum tomatoes
a bunch of cilantro
fresh garlic
a bag of onions
5—6 limons
a bag of lemons
3 ripe avocado pears
a head of lettuce

Mexican oregano
Cumino
turmeric
Serrano and Jalapeno peppers
4 pounds of fresh cut-up chicken
Creme Rancheria
Mexican cheeses
cream cheese
2 pounds of black beans
1 large can of pinto beans
2-pound bag of short-grain rice
3 dozen El Milagro maiz tortillas
corn oil
a large can of chicken broth
1 pound of unsalted butter
5 pounds of unbleached flour
a bottle of pure vanilla extract

and we are all set.

The little one and I head up the path. Projects, chores, responsibilities, appointments, obligations, that heady scent of lilac, Bourbonnais roses, and the remaining narcissus muddle my thoughts. The path from home is not the straight walk it once was. My path is strewn with leaves, stems, flowers, and looming shadows. Veronica Speedwell leans over each side gossiping with Chrysanthemum. The peonies now need their own zip code, but at least the lilies keep to themselves. The black-eyed Susans are spreading everywhere, but the cronewort, *Artemisia vulgaris* (where the hell did *cronewort* come from?), thankfully, is just as thick as she is tall. I hear her cackle coming and going, though sometimes it is just barely audible. She and her feathery leaves looking like helping hands and all. Tough sage green on top, tender, soft, and silver beneath, tassels above all, lending sultry airs all around.

Mysteriously, cronewort has taken up residence outside our front door. Where once there was order, plans, direction to my garden, there is now a lush green space, whose semblance of order lies beneath, at the base of the garden, within the roots. Buried remnants of well-laid plans intermingle with seashells and pennies from days of old. My garden is now a sanctuary. Birds, bees, children, and weary commuters find soul food and solace as they make their way through the world. This place people used to call a yard is now more Healer's Thatch than garden. Approaching a wildflower prairie, this space is sheltered by a teeming forest of sunflowers with the cronewort and her stylish silver tresses acting as gatekeeper.

We head down the path, close the ramshackle gate with its flaking layers of eggshell, which reveal a rich butter-yellow color beneath. Time for li'l boy and me to make our way through the urban forest of elms, oaks, and maples. This local shop is owned and operated by Mexican Americans. As usual, everything we need is ripe, fresh, cheap, and in stock. Tonight we can make wonderfully authentic tacos, enchiladas, and taquitos.

Fait accompli. I gather my flimsy white plastic bags and place them into the shopping cart. This is when I realize my dilemma. I don't have a car and I just spent every dime in my pocket so we can't take a cab. I've got a three-year-old with me. How the hell am I going to carry all of this stuff home? With no inspired answer and an impatient shopper all but shoving me out of the line, I grab up the bags, five per hand, and head out. I've always been strong. Built strong. I've got big bones, broad shoulders, and thick legs to match the willpower. I can do this, right?

Wrong. Each half block, I put the bags down and examine my red-rimmed fingers. I look around with embarrassment at the people perched on their porches; watering their flowers; cutting grass; a few gulp down iced beverages; some gaze my way. Has anyone seen my weakness? I don't know, but the sheer thought that someone might and the promise of Mexican food and limeade followed by shortbread for dessert propels us forward. Half block by half block, we creep home. After about thirty minutes, we've covered about five blocks—only six more to go. I feel wind and hear a rustle behind us—could it be Oya? Not quite. A bouncy, fresh-faced, young woman with blue eyes and blond curly hair bounds up to us. "Need some help?" she queries. Is this a joke? I wonder tiredly. Does she plan to steal our supper? No one helps anyone these days. We can barely help ourselves. Weakness gives her the answer, "Yes, please! Yes, we need some help."

"I haven't seen you around," I say, wondering whether she is one of those angels folks chat about on the *Oprah* show. Her story has an ephemeral quality, uniting her with the heavenly spirit, all the more. "Yeah, just moved to your neighborhood from Iowa. I'm staying with friends [I haven't heard of these folks, though they live a block and a half away] until tomorrow, then I move to my own apartment in the city," she says, as I ponder the fickleness of fate. "My house was surrounded on three sides by farms," she intrudes on my thoughts as melodically as a wind chime. "I walk for a living," she adds. "Doing what?" I query. "Trying to save the earth," she sighs.

Emotions and memories wash over me. The memory of trying to settle into an urban environment after growing up in the wetlands. The all-important goal of finding a job that would make a difference. The anxiety—can I make it in the big city?—The sincere desire to try to help others, even strangers on the street. The boundless energy of youth, when did it leave me? Today I can barely keep up. I am winded. She now has three-quarters of the bags, but she doesn't just walk; she seems to glide along. It is an effort for her to stay grounded, to match my slow pace. Conversation is all that unites us. Suddenly, it is quite evident why the cronewort has taken up residence at my door and why I despise her so.

Usually, I am full of complaints about my tangled mass of stems, overgrown perennials, strangling weeds, and stinging nettles. Now I just want to get home and latch that decrepit gate behind me. No matter that as of this spring the elder boy towers over me and I feel the rustling winds of Oya's skirts as he passes in pursuit of hopes and dreams beyond my reach. Though they are gangly and a bit unruly, still, I know that as each child grows, the *Helianthus annus* will present each of my children's aspirations to the sun. Our toddler and the newly transplanted French lavender (*Lavandula officinalis*), rose-scented geranium (*Pelargonium*, rose like P. Attar of Roses), German chamomile (*Matricaria chamomilla*), and hyssop (*Hyssopus officinalis*) seedlings vie for the warming rays of the sun and merciful light along with a precious bit of space to call their own.

"Wow, is this your garden!" my angel of mercy exclaims. "Oh, are those pink flowers peonies?" she gushes. "Oh, yes, it's all mine—smell the peonies, they are just divine!" I answer with pride. I don't really know why, but suddenly I am overwhelmed with emotion, my eyes are welling up with tears. I am so happy to be home in my garden. "I'm going to make some shortbread tonight, can one of my children bring you some?" I query. "I love shortbread, but I don't need any payment. I just saw you and I thought, man, that woman really needs some help, so I walked as fast as I could to catch up to you." I squeezed her tight and the tears ran freely between our breasts. "Thank you. Thanks a lot!" I mumble. Then, just as deftly as she arrived, she disappears.

Stooping over to lessen the load, the reflection in the puddle reveals a wide-hipped, broad-shouldered black woman, flicks of gray intermingled in her reddish-brown afro. She looks back at me with the fixed gaze of one-who-sees.

Time to stop overlooking the ancient wisdom that has taken root at my doorstep. Tonight I will cut some cronewort down for the first time. I will rub her between my palms, inhale her camphor-like aroma deeply, and then place a bit of her green blood on my third eye, so I can have better foresight. Next, I'll stuff the stems and leaves in a jar and drench them in safflower oil. While I'm waiting for the Crone to release her powers into the oil, I'll do another cutting. This bunch of the feathered Hag will be braided, tied with hemp string, and, once dried, she will be lit. The flames will be snuffed, so only her smoky voice remains, to be waved over the doorstep that she faces and protects. "Crone Wort, bless this path, stoop, and entry and all those who cross this way," I implore in hushed tones by the light of the full moon. Once the moon completes her full cycle, I'll strain a bit of that precious green oil and pour it on my naked body, letting it penetrate my tired soul, aching joints, and Earth-shaped belly. When I am sufficiently healed, I'll work on my soul mate, my children, and others in need.

Time to use what has been given and to realize that I am no longer a slender girl eagerly searching for homes on distant shores.

Woman of the house
planter of seeds
tiller of dreams
Too old to call maiden and too young to call crone.

The Dance of Life

WUANDA M. T. WALLS

It was a typical, brisk, sunny Colorado day when I called my mother to ask about her health. I was living over a thousand miles away from the rolling hills of southeast Pennsylvania, and each season childhood memories would break free and gnaw at my heart. Often, I recalled our clan (grandparents, godparents, uncles, aunts, and cousins) sledding down steep farmland hills, ice skating on the village pond, and enjoying spring and autumn festivities. At times, I imagined myself sitting in the backseat of my parents' convertible, wide-eyed and smiling, enchanted by flowering forsythia, lilac, dogwood, and magnolia during springtime and, in autumn, dazed by brilliant, colorful foliage.

Nevertheless, despite the fact that Pennsylvania's winters were not as harsh as years ago, the season was definitely longer and bleaker than winters in Colorado—a well-kept secret I discovered shortly after I moved to Denver in 1986 and which was confirmed when I realized that the subtle ache in my right knee didn't flare up when the mercury dipped.

On that winter day, I casually asked my mother if she could remember having any aches and pains when she was forty-five. She paused, and answered in a quick, flippant manner. "What are you talking about? I don't have any aches and pains now!"

Surely, I didn't feel old and I was thankful that I was a size six without any medical baggage to worry about, but time catches up with everyone. Thus, my mother's answer didn't sit right with me, and immediately my tone became flat and saucy.

"Mom, you know what I mean. Did you notice any changes in your body?"

She replied in that sly, impassive way, which exemplified her strength. "No, I never get headaches, don't catch colds, I don't suffer from allergies, and I don't have ulcers. I'm really blessed and I thank the Lord every day for my health and strength."

Lord knows, I had heard those words enough to know what was coming next. Then, she said it. "You must take care of yourself. Remember to always do everything in moderation."

Suddenly, as if for the first time, I knew how fortunate she was. She had inherited her paternal ancestors' genes. A combination of her grandmother, Mary Ellen Harris-Tittle (b. 4/9/1868), and her grandfather, George Washington Tittle (b. 9/22/1858), well-to-do farmers who were born in the Old Line state of Maryland, where the Mason and Dixon Line became not only the boundary between Pennsylvania and Maryland, but between North and South, freedom and slavery. Fortunately, they lived in western Maryland, a stone's throw away from Pennsylvania, where whites' and free African Americans' status rested securely on land holdings. Both were of sturdy African, Native American, and European stock, reputed for their enterprising natures, progressive minds, tenacity, stamina, and longevity. On the other hand, many of her maternal ancestors died in middle age of cancer, including her mother, Bertha, who died at fifty-three. And the reality of Bertha's death left my mother distraught and fearful of cancer. Fears that caused her to believe she would die in the prime of her life.

Before our telephone conversation ended on that winter day, I reflected on her good health, her fears, and losses. What stood out were her losses, for she had suffered many since her mother's death. The most significant being the loss of her loving and devoted husband, who died of a heart attack in 1977. For a couple of months after he died, she would leave her bed and walk down the steps to his playground, the basement. It was his pride and joy, especially the bar built in collaboration with his uncle and his drinking buddies. The walls were decorated with sports pennants, record album covers, postcards from their travels, and travel posters. And it smelled of cigarette, cigar, and pipe tobacco, marked by gay times gone stale.

Broken and mortally wounded, nothing loving or generous seemed to direct her life any longer. In her eyes, I saw her grief, sorrow, loneliness, and fears. Often, I sensed her need for my company, compassion, and understanding, but at times, I was unable to give of myself on her terms. After all, I thought, I was grieving, too. Eventually, the thought of living life without her husband wore her down. She stopped eating, lost weight, and closed the door on life, as it were. Nevertheless, at fifty-four she was still attractive, graceful, and vital. And months later, she began to venture out into the world. Her first bold steps took her to New Mexico. There, she was embraced by her dear friend Muriel and Muriel's family, and it was the perfect tonic, for she and my dad had vacationed there in the 1960s and loved it.

Travel came easy for them for it was a shared passion. Now, without her mate, she was able to find solace in new landscapes, seascapes, and nature, as well as in old stomping grounds and familiar faces. However, liberty without companionship was difficult and seemed unnatural at first, but the healing process had begun.

Eleven years later, in 1989, when spring approached, I was preoccupied with preparations for her visit. I had visited Pennsylvania in the fall and was anxious to see her. She was also excited, and we planned her itinerary over the phone. Denver was a favorite destination. She loved the city, the people, and the mountains. That year she came with her friend Connie, and our first stop was to the Indian Springs Resort. Nestled in the Rockies, the mineral spring hot pools contain iron, magnesium, zinc, sulfate, and other beneficial minerals known for their healing properties. After several minutes in the pool, our skin tingled without warning and our muscles relaxed. Mom's face was rosy and aglow.

She looked radiant. When we left, our bodies and spirits felt completely replenished.

Loving my mother made me proud. A woman endowed with a warm, sensitive, generous, and compassionate heart. Our bond was like the Möbius strip I often wore around my neck, one-sided, yet intertwining. We had a close mother-daughter relationship, an open, honest friendship, which embodied admiration. Notwithstanding, my mother was not perfect. Often this truth caused me to analyze the complexity of the woman, who at times was baffling. Ardelle could be firm, temperamental, domineering, unforgiving, vain, and seductive. She possessed the maternal softness of soul mixed with the strength of a lioness.

Over the years, we had our differences. Heated disagreements in which we exchanged words lip to lip and unreasonable standstills rooted in pride, selfishness, and control. There were even periods when we stopped speaking and didn't visit; those were turbulent years when I was becoming my own woman—sure, confident, and rebellious. But throughout it all, she never condemned me nor did she try to hold on. She knew she had done her best.

It was during those intense times that I focused on the stories about her childhood, her family, her romantic escapades, and my birth. The stories helped me to put things in perspective as I tried to understand the woman . . . not the mother. Naturally, I was never bored with my birth story. She would look at me with those same expressive, deepening eyes of her mother, smile a tender smile and begin.

"When I felt the labor pains, I was afraid and I didn't want to go to the hospital, so I kept quiet. Your dad's grandmother Jessie and your great Aunt Reba knew it was time and called my father. Your dad was working miles away, so Pop and Mom drove me nearly twenty miles to Chester County Hospital. You were delivered by your grandfather's cousin, Dr. Orville Walls. Before I saw you, the nurses told me you were perfect and beautiful. Finally, I saw you. I couldn't believe my eyes. Your eyes were magnificent, as black as coal, mysterious, and bright. Black curly locks covered your head and you had the cheekbones of your African and Indian ancestors. The nurses kept coming in to see you. I felt like a queen. And I named you after a dear friend, a white woman I met while working one summer at the shore. Later, I became possessive. Everywhere we went, people commented on your eyes, your beauty, and wanted to touch you. I was obsessed, thinking something awful was going to happen to you." Consequently, I became a shy, clingy baby, possessing her features and temperament.

During her visit that spring, she did not retell my birth story but delighted me with family updates and her own tales of life. She appeared healthy and happy, but a few times she jokingly said that she was getting older, which I thought uncharacteristic, but no big deal. However, several months later, when I asked her to plan her next visit she refused.

"I think you should visit me more," she replied.

"Okay, I will. But I know how much you like Denver, the climate, and the mineral springs."

"Yes, I do. But your mother is getting older. Besides, I don't know if I want to fly anymore. There have been so many accidents lately."

I recoiled, almost compelled to say, bah, don't give me that. But instead, I said in a playful manner, "Oh, come on, Mom, you know you aren't afraid of flying; you're too feisty. Now, tell me, is there a new love on the horizon?"

I sensed that she repressed a chuckled before she said, "Well, we'll see. Now, when are you coming?"

Although my concern about her grew stronger and stronger, I knew not to pressure her to visit, and before I knew it, a year had passed. As time went on, I noticed that she didn't call as often and she couldn't remember when I called last. The telltale signs of memory loss were subtle but poignant, and I was unnerved. A deep need to be near her and to assist gripped me. During our phone conversations, I listened for cues signaling that she was headed for the realm of Alzheimer's. This was indeed disturbing and painful because I knew most of her paternal ancestors succumbed to senility. Yes, longevity was on their side but their minds moved into another dimension.

Soon, I began to think of ways to entice her to move to Denver. After all, she loved the West and my support network was tremendous. She had met many people her age with common interests and often said she would like to spend six months or more in Denver. But deep down I knew to uproot her from her family, church, neighbors, beloved friends, and companion would be detrimental. Besides, if I was with her, I could share more of my knowledge about herbal therapy, acupuncture, and massage therapy and also cook her wholesome vegetarian meals.

In 1992, I decided to spend a month with her. It was a fun-filled month but things were different. My stylish Mom had stopped wearing makeup, and at night she forgot to remove her dentures. Her culinary skills were also diminishing, and my favorite meals tasted bland and looked unappealing. How could this be, I thought, as I remembered her kitchen as the place where she reigned supreme, preparing splendid meals with love and joy. In the past, savory dishes of baked macaroni and cheese, baked shad, veal cutlets, chicken and dumplings, and potatoes prepared countless ways (mashed, creamed, scalloped, fried, baked, and boiled) would grace the table in a snap.

I covered up my growing concern and sadness during the day, but alone in my bed at night I ransacked my mind over the fact that the handwriting was on the wall. My mother was aging. And as painful as it was, I had to accept it. My heartstrings ached when it was time to leave. And as I waved good-bye, I looked past her smile and tried not to read her mind. What do you think of me now? What's on your mind? What's in your heart? I studied her face for a brief moment, realizing her beauty was new and strange. She was no longer robust, voluptuous, and energetic. But her delicate frame captivated me, as she and her companion waved and blew kisses. At once, with my back to the wind, I shook and broke out in tears.

Several months later, I decided to move back home. Fortunately, I was blessed with the support of everyone, and, to honor my decision, my friends held ceremonies to sanctify the natural cycle of life. Each ceremony, each thought of good-bye pained my heart. My emotions were topsy-turvy and I wavered; holding on to a desired lifestyle, a place of serenity and spiritual manna, while preparing to embrace the womb of love.

At midlife, the time had come for me to caress my mother at dusk, and I believed every twist and turn in my life had prepared me for this. My travels, contact with other cultures, marriage, miscarriages, my personal relationship with God, love of nature, the arts, and my deep, intimate friendships.

Yes, she had slowed down a bit, but so had I. Besides, she was still beautiful, vibrant, healthy, and active. For me, it was important to satisfy my need to be close to her, to drink in time. To eat together, pray together, travel together, live together once again . . . to enjoy the dance of life.

Full Circling

ELAINE LEE

What we call the beginning is often the end
And to make an end is to make a beginning.
The end is where we start from.

— *T. S. Eliot*, Four Quartets

I remember the moment on June 5, 2000, when my mother looked at me and said, "Laneruth, I don't think I am going to make it to my birthday." We were in my car en route to one of our favorite Thai restaurants for lunch. While waiting at a stoplight, her proclamation ushered forth with such an odd, calm conviction that it was almost as if she were discussing the weather.

"Why do you think that, Mom?" I asked uneasily, praying she was wrong.

"There is something happening in my body that I have never felt before."

After a year of hopefulness and resiliency in the face of myriad medical interventions and her steady decline, it was only then, six days before her eighty-eighth birthday, that the imminence of her death finally broke through my denial.

Serving as midwife to her transition during those last twelve months, I had steadily assumed increasing responsibility for her care as I witnessed her body and soul slowly transfigure before my eyes. We would often jokingly say in unison, "turnaround is fair play," as we reminisced about the day she brought me home after I was delivered as an abandoned infant into her loving care. Now, I was taking care of her, my mother child, helping her to prepare for her return journey, back to the Source.

The "great undoing" began on the eve of her March 1999 trip

back to Michigan. She was heading home after her annual snow-bird stay with me in California. I gave her a surprise going away party at her favorite Italian restaurant. Little did I know that the party's sweet farewell was a hallmark of the beginning of the end.

Mom had only been back in Michigan a week when she landed in the hospital with a bout of congestive heart failure. I suspect the flight and the residual March winter weather were too much for her. Or perhaps it was the spring cleaning (which always included her favorite chore of moving all of the furniture around). Or maybe it was the combination of all three.

I immediately caught a plane to Michigan, and my surprise visit to her hospital room lifted our troubled spirits. Together, we figured we could handle just about anything. We always had before. I slipped back into my role of managing her health care. Her doctor told me that she was recovering nicely and would be returning home in a few days. That would give me time to get the apartment ready, get food prepared and medications in order.

When I entered the senior citizens apartment complex where she lived, it felt like old home week. The residents and staff warmly welcomed me as I made my way through the foyer and lounge. Many of them seemed to be sitting in exactly the same places as they had been the year before. The resident manager pulled me aside and quietly whispered in my ear that Eddie, Mom's best friend, sent word that she wanted me to stop by her apartment. So, I went to see her.

As soon as we'd finished the welcoming formalities, Eddie laid her cards on the table. "Your eighty-six-year-old mother can no longer manage her life, her finances, or her medicine. And she has no business driving that car you bought her." I was shocked. My mom had just spent three months in my home and I hadn't noticed anything unusual, other than her memory slipping a bit, and her disposition growing a bit more cantankerous. More than a little shaken, I thanked Eddie for her candor and listened intently as she shared the details of my mother's unmanageable life. As the discussion progressed, it became clear to me that my mother was in serious trouble.

Afterward, when I entered her apartment, I was struck by the numerous pictures of me in every room, hung and tacked on the walls, framed and sitting on tabletops and shelves. It had a hint of a shrine, which belied her cool, easygoing, nongushy style of love. I recalled how my dad used to tease her in front of me when I came home for my visits from college about how she "ran around like crazy," cooking, cleaning, and getting things ready, but as soon as I walked in the door, she was suddenly "all laid back" and mellow. Like an actress feigning nonchalance to disguise how thrilled she was that I was home again. Now I discovered that her most recent role during her stay with me was that of the capable, self-reliant, independent woman. It had been a seamless, all-front, and no-back performance piece.

Going through her neatly organized antique secretariat, I discovered the mismanagement of her financial affairs to which Eddie had alluded. And I knew that our lives were about to change profoundly.

After my mother was released from the hospital, I got her situated, her meds in order, her doctor's appointments lined up and rallied friends and family to help with her transportation. Then I headed back to a life that was once mine, but was about to become hers. I was faced with a decision that so many middle-age women have faced in similar situations . . . whether to quit my good job and move back to Michigan or move her to California to be near me. My financial planner helped me figure out a way to finance my new lifestyle as a full-time caregiver. To my surprise, I discovered that if I followed her advice, I could manage for six months to a year.

A month or so later, the universe blessed me with a part-time summer job that allowed me to work from Michigan, where I could live with my mom, help settle her affairs, and explore the idea of moving her to California. Shortly thereafter, my father, who I believe is one of my guardian angels, serendipitously "arranged" for me to meet my first boyfriend in ten years. I met Phillip on Memorial Day, a day I always dedicated to the memory of my long-deceased father. Phillip subsequently fell in love with me and my mom and got a package deal. He committed himself to helping take care of us through hell or high water. "Lawd" knows, he got plenty of both.

I spent the summer arranging my mother's doctors visits, hospitalizations, organizing her financial and legal affairs, which included the unpleasant task of selling the family home and relocating her seventy-eight-year-old tenant, who just happened to be one of her best friends.

Perhaps the most challenging part of all was administering CPR to her when she would occasionally lose her ability to breathe. It was terrifying to see her gasping for air. I was so grateful that the CPR skills she taught our grade school Girl Scout troop actually helped me save her life on several occasions.

Despite the seemingly endless array of life challenges, we remained strong and undaunted, trudging along together from crisis to crisis. Dancing on the edges of life, we somehow managed to distance ourselves from the concept of death, living as if this were a condition that would pass, perhaps opening new possibilities for the future of our little family.

At the end of those three months, having worked tirelessly to pull things together, I convinced myself that it was OK to go back to the Bay Area to my so-called life and to prepare for my mother's move to California. She would remain in Michigan under the watchful eyes of trusted friends and church members, and I also arranged for biweekly visits from a home health care nurse. My mother was insulted by my protective maneuvers, which she swore she didn't need. But it was the only way I could leave her and feel that she was safe.

Two weeks after I left, my mother went back into the hospital again for a blockage in an artery. Luckily, the problem was resolved by a small surgical procedure and she was able to return home within a few days. And with the support network I had arranged before leaving, she was able to manage for the next month or so until I brought her out to California.

Meanwhile, I secured her a lovely, one-bedroom, ocean-view apartment in a brand-new, state-of-the-art senior citizens' complex that was replete with a full-scale health center, an activity center, and a comprehensive range of services. To my delight, it was only a mile from my house.

When Mom arrived at the San Francisco airport, Phillip and I welcomed her through the gate in my customary manner with a fanfare of flowers, balloons, and confetti. People thought she was a celebrity as we paraded through the airport. She was happy, vibrant, and looked quite healthy, but within two days of her flight to California she was hospitalized again with congestive heart failure.

"Laneruth," she asked me, lying in her hospital bed, "am I dying?"

"No, Mom," I told her, believing what I hoped was true. "There are a few more things these highfalutin' California doctors are going to try." And try they did. They administered batteries of tests, sampled new medications and therapies, and consulted numerous specialists.

During those next few months, through a remarkable alchemy of denial, faith, and love, we lived a relatively normal life. Despite two more hospitalizations and dozens of doctor visits, we threw a huge party for our California friends. And Mom elevated herself to the status of "gumbo queen" by making the biggest and tastiest pot of gumbo she had ever made. After that, we returned to Michigan to fetch the rest of her belongings and say her good-byes to friends and family. Upon our return, I had her things moved into her new apartment, opened up a bank account for her, and put her car up for sale. She even planted a large vegetable and herb garden.

Just as we were each getting our new life under way, her physical decline began to accelerate. She had trouble breathing, eating, and sleeping, and she was growing more dependent on her cane. Perhaps all of the changes and the travel were too much. Perhaps it was simply her time. Then came that ominous moment when she looked at me and said, "Laneruth, I don't think I am going to make it to my birthday."

I immediately arranged for her to see her cardiologist. Regretfully, he confirmed her suspicion and admitted her to the intensive care unit. No denial stood between us now. We both knew that barring a miracle, death would soon part us. In our typical way, we lived our last few days together as normally as possible. Four days later, on June 9, 2000, my mother made her transition from the physical plane. The strength, courage, and fearlessness she demonstrated during her final days were a testament to her faith and character. I watched her soul come loose, rumble around, and finally break free from its fleshly form. It moved out of her body and into a powerfully present spirit-self. I pray that her return to the Source was a peaceful and safe journey and that she was met by a welcoming and loving presence.

We, two women, had served one another as faithful stewards at life's two gates . . . at the beginning and at the end. Nature, in its perfect balance, had long ago united a barren wife and a forsaken baby girl. And now I, her barren daughter, mothered her back to the Source.

Between these gates of life and death we had created a forty-seven-year-old world of our design in which honesty, responsibility, punctuality, respect, and reverence ruled. A relationship that left little room for "By the way, I'm sorry," "Oh, but I was too tired," "I didn't mean it," or "Hey, but I tried." Don't get me wrong: we had our issues, and our issues had issues, but they were a small fragment of our life together, which held a rich, unwavering, overflowing love that was sealed with the pact "Be on my side, I'll be on your side." Now that long-familiar world we made had come to an end.

As my mother predicted, on June 11, 2000, I celebrated her eighty-eighth birthday without her. In honor of her life and her passing, I created an altar in my house. I draped a colorful kente cloth over a small wooden table on which I placed a vase of fresh flowers, some candles, my favorite pictures of her, and a small basket with some of her favorite belongings, including her wedding ring, car keys, Girl Scout pin, eyeglasses, and a few framed scriptures and poems. To honor her memory, and that of my other ancestors, I made a vow to keep fresh flowers and a burning candle on the altar and to say a daily prayer for her.

I garner some comfort from the circumstances of her last year. She lived and died on her own terms, a remarkably free woman. She didn't die alone, she was never an invalid, never in a nursing home, and she didn't have to say good-bye to me. She hated good-byes.

And I now know that the end of a life is not the end of a relationship. Our bond has shape-shifted into new and ever-changing forms. I regularly experience her via dreams, visions, animals, nature, and remarkable coincidences. I catch glimpses of her in other people's faces, hear her voice in other people's laughter, and witness her in me. Like the other day, when I looked around my house at all the pictures and artifacts of her and thought to myself, "Chile', you sho' is yo mutha's dawta," as I was reminded of how her apartment had been full of pictures of me. I often channel her energy when I am cooking. After serving as her culinary apprentice for many decades, I learned to replicate her cooking wizardry and to skillfully recreate many of her favorite dishes, to the delight and amazement of my friends.

In the period after her passing, I often told myself, "Don't cry because her life is over, smile because her life happened." This helped to sustain me during the dismantling and disposing of the material world my mother had left behind, especially the surreal aspect as she went from a person, to a nonperson, to an inanimate object, and then into a conglomeration of tasks, duties, and obligations to be handled and attended to. With the help of family, friends, and my bereavement group, I found the strength to deal with them all, including but not limited to making arrangements for the cremation; writing the obituary; designing, producing, and sending a memorial booklet to family and friends; preparing and executing the estate sale; distributing keepsakes to her inner circle; dealing with those ornery folks at the social security and pension offices as well as with the subsequent tragic death of her dog (I suspect he died of a broken heart).

This profusion of tasks in the wake of her passing confounded the sense of loss of the person who had been the central figure of my life. And having spent almost every day of the past year caring for her, I was left with an empty space in my life, my home, and my heart. Facing me, concomitantly, was the task of rebuilding my emotional and material life without her love, encouragement, and abiding faith in my abilities. At the ripe middle age of forty-eight, I was being called upon to rebirth myself and learn for the first time to be my own best friend and to draw from myself that faith, love, and strength for life that I had always drawn from her.

In celebration of her life and her love, I produced a memorial concert (she did not want a funeral). Titled "Crossing Over: An Evening of Music, Ritual, and Meditation in Honor of the Lives and Deaths of Our Mothers," it featured the music of inspirational performing artist Kathy Zavada, whose music celebrates love, peace, and the blessed union between mothers and daughters and incorporates the imagery of the divine ascended mother. It was held at an exquisitely beautiful recital hall that was lavishly decorated with bouquets of flowers and balloons as well as an altar on which each of the seventy attendees placed pictures of their mothers and lit a candle in her honor. There were numerous works of art displayed around the hall from my bereavement art class, and, holding court in the front row, was a large, stunningly beautiful ethnic-style rag doll a textile artist friend of mine and I cocreated using Mom's favorite African dress and jewelry. After the event and its reception, we held a balloon launch in the adjoining courtyard, where we each released to the sky a helium-filled balloon in honor of our mothers. The evening's program provided us a wonderful way to collectively celebrate our women ancestors.

The vegetable garden my mom planted a week before she died produced a bountiful harvest that summer and continued to yield crops through the next January. Eating the vegetables from her garden became a kind of holy communion for me. The circle remains unbroken — death is not the end, and birth is not the beginning. They are only the transitions in God's great wheel of life.

In the Heat of Shadow

JEWELLE GOMEZ

A gallery of photographs has adorned the walls of my various apartments since I left the Boston home of my great-grandmother in 1971 to live in New York City. Each of the faces—my mother, Dolores; her mother, Lydia; her mother Grace, and yet another, Sarah, before her; alongside my great-grandfather, father, half-brother, and stepmother—has in its own turn been a focal point for me. Most often, though, it has been the face of my great-grandmother Grace, the woman who raised me, that I found most fascinating. She who was always most reticent to have her soul captured on a piece of shining paper. Her square Ioway tribal face was often shielded by wire spectacles that concealed her impish humor but not her unyielding resolve. From my childhood perspective (one I've clung to until recently), she embodied the security of my youth, the impressive influence of our past, and the endurance of African/Native American women.

Her daughter, Lydia, with whom I've been most close in the past ten years, represented the possibilities of talent and beauty. In the pictures her face shines with charm, intelligence, and sensuality. I never dress, sing, kiss, teach, or sew without seeing that face, for she was the one who taught me those things. But she died in the summer of 1988. I haven't been able to place that loss yet; she's still alive in so much that I do.

It's the face of my mother Dolores that holds my eye now as I feel the chilly departure of youth. Hers is a face of uncertainty, the unknown. Although it is clear we are all descendants of Sarah, whom I never knew, Dolores and I grow ever closer in resemblance each year. Her portrait among the others is arch, sophisticated, distant, like many done of glamorous women in the early 1950s. I can see the painted line of her eyebrow, the deliberate softness of her jaw line, the romanticized wave of her hair. In the corner her inscription to me is still faintly visible in the dramatic script I was so used to deciphering in her letters to me when I was a child. What shocks me is that I am now older than my mother was when she gave up custody of me in 1954 and inscribed this photo as a remembrance. I don't know what makes me suddenly afraid except perhaps that she was clearly a "woman" in this picture. She represented adulthood, something children can never really reach. Instead we shed our skins and one day awaken to be another person—the adult. The continuity between child and adult is indiscernible to me—the continuum seems tentative, as if we hopscotched through our lives landing solidly in certain ages and less certainly in others. Who was I at eleven or twenty-six, the age my mother is in the picture?

Dolores always seemed as solid as Grace or Lydia in her self-knowledge and self-determination. It is only later that I came to realize this was not true. Her life was a mass of contradictions, missteps, youthful inadequacies, none so different from my shortcomings at twenty-six. But I have no child to judge my photograph.

It is her face that confuses me, that worries me as I step into what they call middle age. My misunderstanding of who my mother was as an adult and my clear understanding of how our culture's definition of middle-aged life has changed for most women combine to leave me unsatisfied about my future—even terrified of it. I know some women who cannot allow their lives to be changed by the redefinitions of middle age that have been wrought by the Black Power and women's movements. There is always a certain investment in the traditional even when it is despairing and oppressive. Many women still cling to the comforting stereotypes, as if they can transform themselves into Pearl Bailey or Donna Reed—either good-natured complainants or models of sweet contentment. I have cousins now, only thirty years old, who, burdened with children and missing boyfriends, take easy refuge in the myth of middle-aged behavior. They in their youth know the speech and behavioral patterns, the postures so well, it's haunting in its familiarity. It's like watching them reenact scenes from old TV shows— *Good Times, The Jeffersons, Amos and Andy.*

One aspect of traditional African American culture has provided us with a couple of solid pictures of who we grow up to be. The long-suffering matriarch who gathers her extended family to her bosom and regales them with the stories of her exciting yet simple girlhood, the things they are missing because they don't exist anymore. She is revered much like my stepmother, Henrietta, who at seventy-one has spent her life raising other people's children with a wit and graciousness unmatched by anyone I've ever met. Her life settled down into middle age, then old age, with appointed purpose—children. Her role as a caretaker almost required her to be middle aged in order to be acceptable, so she may have started becoming middle-aged at age thirty like my cousins, those she raised.

On the other side of the myth stand Dolores and Lydia, women who had little contact with the idea of middle age. Their lives moved ahead as if there were only eternity, and the road map had been given directly into their hands. At family gatherings I didn't hear the discussions of middle-aged discontent, the things undone, the anxiety, confinement, or unfulfillment. They seemed to take advancing age as only one other element to be included in their daily calculations, like rain or high wind. None of them allowed their lives to be bound up in the lives of their children, so the crises attendant to that link and its dissolution were barely visible. My great-grandmother took the news of my decision to move away from home after college with amazing equanimity. I'm sure she didn't disclose the sadness it brought her because she thought that inappropriate to the natural order. When I did move I called her on the telephone every day, unafraid to declare my love and my missing her because she didn't represent a trap laid to ensnare me, luring me back to the nest. She seemed to be a woman going on with her life. The few months that remained for her at age eighty-eight included a visit to me in Manhattan as if she wanted to really give me her blessing.

Now, for me at forty, having no children, no property, living in the nontraditional roles of lesbian/feminist, African American, and Native American writer under the enigmatic gaze of my mother, I am frightened by the prospect of middle age. If I reject the traditional perception of who I am, what do I replace it with? I've no idea. My mind says there's really no limit. I write, I remain committed as a progressive activist; I'm continually building friendships. What is there to be afraid of? Most of it seems to be physical. My body doesn't move for me as it used to. While the exercise craze has hit the lesbian community with equal if not larger force than in the general society, I've managed to evade the compunction to rise at dawn and run through city streets or submit to the rack masquerading as a Nautilus device. So, I may be in worse shape than some but I refuse to feel guilty about it. My body aches and is stiff. It does not heal. It mocks me with its readiness to become old. But there is a certain amount of comfort in that too. My body has relieved me of the obligation to pursue daring physical feats. Will I ever learn to ski? Do I care?

But it really isn't the body—it's the replacement image. There is none. I'm not washed up, at the end of my rope, over the hill, on the decline, or any of the other euphemisms, at least not overtly. But what am I? I keep looking at Dolores's picture—the quizzical line of her brow, the directness of her gaze. There is something there, I think, which might tell me of a new opening, even if it is one she might have lost sight of. She cannot be dismissed because she had a penchant for falling in love with braggarts with unrealistic visions of life. The issues I had, still have, with my mother (about politics and hair care mostly) sometimes overwhelm the practical love I feel for her. As powerful as these issues are they cannot overshadow what I see in that look. Are there answers there? I am as uncertain about that as the future her look promises. What do I have that will allow me to look back at others with such self-possession?

I take some comfort in my "professional status," that is, the publication of my work and my audience's appreciation of it. That is a gift not available to many women. But to identify myself only as what I do is a mistake that men have made too often throughout history. But what do I make of myself embarking on a new and serious relationship at forty, with little of the romanticism of the previous twenty years' debacles, but more of the practicality of a diplomatic negotiator?

It may simply be the fear that all feminists must face: how to balance the power of control over my own life with a need for support and encouragement. The women in my family seemed to be able to handle only one of these things at a time. My mother let her life be subsumed under those of her partners. She chose gregarious, charming men who controlled the shape of both their lives, while her prime function was to maintain a full-time job and still look pampered.

My grandmother, Lydia, landed at the other extreme. She allowed men to enter her life for prescribed periods of time for her own enjoyment. When they became too intrusive they were banished back to their own apartments, their own lives. She repeated this process through her middle years with a sort of stable of men who never seemed to tire of her attentions and rejections. She was extraordinarily clear about her independence and managed to forsake most expressions of need, as if the two could not cohabit within her any more than she could cohabitate with a man for more than six months.

The ache in my knees and hands makes me certain I don't want to give up the right to supportive companionship, any more than I'd consider becoming anyone's appendage. And it is entering the middle years—the aches and uncertainty—that makes the questions more pointed. I want my answer to be somewhere in my mother's face but more likely it is in the faces of both Dolores and Lydia. The balancing act is what I'm afraid of. My body and ego feel particularly fragile now while they are in transition from a solid past to an unknown future. Taking to the high wire to figure out where I'm strong and where I'm needy feels like stretching my resources too far. And I've always been afraid of heights.

Taken all together, the portraits of the women in my family have been a great sustainer over the years of my adulthood. Each in its own turn has meant something specific, has conveyed some particular lesson that I've needed to learn in order to move on to the next phase of my development. The part that I'd not reckoned with is the reverse side of the coin: the lineage and triumph that the women of my family represent is also a burden. They did not express themselves in the same womanly ways that I do. Even with a fantastical imagination and knowing their iconoclastic natures I can't picture Dolores going braless or Lydia devising dreadlocks out of her Ioway/Wampanoag hair.

They were less likely to articulate who they were and what they envisioned as the definitions of their lives. As heterosexual women coming of age in the 1920s, '30s, and '40s this was not required of them. In fact, such expression was discouraged because they were women and because they were not white. That silence, even as I take courage from their examples, is a curtain between me and what my life after forty can be. And because they survived so magnificently, with such style and humor, they have become legend to me. Their pictures are icons enshrined in the nave of my apartment, lending inspiration—but also casting a shadow.

I begin to see that my life cannot be fully patterned on theirs, if simply because it's decades later socially, politically, and economically; if only because I am a lesbian and they were not lesbians. But the shadow projected by their lives still hangs there and it is not cool. It is hot with expectation. It makes me sweat as I climb onto the high wire and learn what happens when I try to see what a colored lesbian looks like when she lives longer than the statistics say she should. And I'm still afraid of heights.

Further Reflections—Eleven Years Later

I moved into my new home with my partner, Diane, in 1993 and one of the ways I still settle into a place is putting up the photographs of my family. The rogues' gallery my grandmother, Lydia, called it. And some of them do look like rogues, at least in my mind's eye, because I know many of the stories behind their images. They were never afraid to appear human and fallible before me. I've always looked like each of them in a variety of ways, some, small, some quite obvious. And at the age of almost fifty-four I look more and more like their sister rather than their daughter or granddaughter.

The past few years have been the most difficult of any I've lived through as a conscious adult. I don't suppose they're as traumatizing as when your mother dumps you on unknown relatives when you're two years old (as mine did). These traumas are the ones we've been told to expect: getting older, losing friends, facing mortality.

But as an adult the measure of who I am has become less connected to the pictures of others and more grounded in my own life.

The pictures of my family still mean a great deal to me. They are both the sunshine and the shadow beneath which I've lived my entire life. But I come to see that they are not really a reflection of who I'm meant to be. My own friends, my own stories have begun to frame the image I see. I can remember my grandmother lamenting the death of her close friends as she got older. Now I find myself doing the same. When Audre Lorde died in 1992 my grief was somewhat short-circuited by the fact that I had to write her obituary for *Essence* magazine. But sitting alone at home after I'd mailed off my copy, I was left holding the beaded necklace she had made for me. The public nature of Audre's death did not ameliorate the emptiness I felt inside. Nor did it stay the fear that arose naturally: if she can die, then so too will I and not in some distant future. And then the others: June Jordan, Barbara Christian, Gwendolyn Brooks, Shirley Anne Williams. Having friends die who will be mourned by millions doesn't really make you feel any better. And the private deaths—my childhood friends, those I hear about at my high school reunion, or the many who died from HIV infection—they reflect my mortality just as sharply as the deaths of my more famous friends.

But now I know that only inspiration, not answers, are what I can look for in the pictures of my relatives. It is in the lives of my contemporaries, those who've gone ahead and passed before me and those who keep living beside me, that may be the net beneath that high wire. We all have stories of people who've done extraordinary things—survived poverty, illness, war. And many of them have done it not just as an individual triumph but have found ways to make their success count in the lives of others. And many of them have managed to maintain good humor, a wide worldview and curiosity about things. At this point most of my friends put a time limit on how long we'll allow ourselves to complain about menopause, joint pain, or passing friends. But what matters for me is that we can take that allotted time, complain like hell, then really get back to a major conversation.

The commonality in my generation—that of the baby boomers, a phrase I hate—is a sense of flexibility. We marched in protest when we were nineteen; but we could also do it (and sometimes do) today. We're in it for the long haul. Social change, a glimmer of which I recognized in the eyes of the women of my family, is part of the fabric of our beliefs. There is a quote from Chief Joseph of the Nez Perce: let us put our heads together and see what kind of world we can make for our children. That means we have to be flexible in order to recognize what actual social change is and what is just more of the same.

In the moments when I used to gaze at the photographs of my mother and grandmother I didn't often think about what their lives were like in that moment, when they were young. I saw them as fully formed. Now I see them as both the young women they were and the old women they became. What I admire is how they managed to keep being themselves. The flexibility that was part of who they were made it possible for Lydia to be progressive at eighty and for Dolores to call my partner, Diane, her daughter.

I will never learn to ski, walk on an actual high wire (no matter how much money a reality show offers), or some of the other things that women of fifty-four love to do. That's just not me. But the middle years are when everything—body and beliefs—starts to stiffen, to harden, and I've learned to be on guard against that. I have to imagine myself as both young and old in order to keep growing into who I am and keep the brain and joints moving. The changes in the world I'd like to see happen are not for my generation alone. In order to believe they're possible I have to assume that the change will be for generations to come and that I am not the only one who defines what that'll look like.

The unfortunate thing about the photographs I've gazed upon

all these years is that they're still; they don't capture the energy and action of life. It was really the movement of those women that was amazing. Grace walking the mile to the market every Saturday morning with a firm step until she could walk no more, Lydia's fingers flying over the strings of her guitar trying to keep arthritis at bay, Dolores lifting a woman from her wheelchair to get her up the stairs to Christmas Eve mass, cursing the lack of a ramp. I see their energy and action in those I've chosen to be my friends and family today. That flexibility of mind, body, and spirit are what I was really recognizing when I looked at the women in my family. It's what I hope to see in myself.

Parents, Wives, and Womanhood: The Lessons We Never Learned

Ta'SHIA ASANTI KARADE

I'd heard it said that when a woman approaches midlife everything starts to make sense. Life becomes a series of "light bulb" moments in which clarity to make decisions in one's best interest is gained and decisions become easier and easier. But it wasn't until I turned forty that I realized age is not just a number, it's a turning point, a biological and spiritual guidepost to life experiences. Don't get me wrong, midlife isn't some magic wand that renders one protected from future mistakes. However, it does provide a substantial view of the paths that won't produce happiness and inner fulfillment. For me the lessons were vast. I'd made plenty of mistakes and had come to realize that my role in those errors was what needed evaluating. After doing so, I began the journey of correcting my mistakes, starting with the inside of me.

My first lesson was with my daughter, who had recently turned twenty-one, a beautiful young woman with a liberal amount of self-will that had caused much of the pain in our lives. In fact, my daughter's mistakes had cost me unnecessary money, physically damaging stress, and nights of lost sleep. And, of course, these mistakes were mostly in areas in which I had given her guidance that she refused to follow. After she bailed out on me to take a road trip with her then-boyfriend while I was left to care for my ailing mother alone, I realized I had to make some changes in the way we related. She was no longer a child deserving of a one-sided relationship. It was time for our relationship to transition into an exchange, one in which we supported each other. Certainly, I'd never completely depend on her, or anyone else for that matter, for my emotional support. However, she was now old enough to love me back. I realized that it was unhealthy to be hurt and disappointed on a continual basis by anyone, even my own child. Altering our relationship wasn't about withholding my love and support, it was about sharing it in a way that wouldn't deplete me or make me feel used. The change only strengthened our relationship and increased my love for myself. Most important, it taught my daughter that parents have feelings too.

The next big lesson was in pursuing my goals. I was in a wonderful marriage that had faced minor challenges in the four short years we'd been together. After a series of unhealthy relationships, I truly treasured my relationship. I didn't dare take a chance on messing it up. But there was a significant part of me that I felt driven to give up in order to maintain my marriage, the part that wanted to be a successful writer. I desperately wanted to apply for fellowships in creative writing at a university in another state. If I got accepted, it would mean being away from home for as long as a year. I feared the impact this would have on my marriage. I feared the impact that not applying would have on my spirit.

My mate was incredibly supportive of my career as a writer and would never stand in the way of my professional or personal growth. I was torn between the two loves in my life, my writing and my life partner. But the lesson here wasn't to abandon my spouse for my career or to abandon my dreams. The lesson was to learn to find a middle ground — one that would allow me to remain loyal to my vision and goals and to my marriage. I searched for and found a shorter fellowship; it was actually a residence at a retreat center for women. There, I could have the peace and solitude to complete my novel and continue to nurture my loveship. Prior to entering midlife, my disease to please would've directed me to abandon my dream of finishing my novel in lieu of service to someone else. Experience has taught me that love of self must come first if you want to have and keep the love of others. People will treat you exactly how you treat yourself. And the blessings of life and living just keep getting better.

The last big lesson was the most important of all. It was the lesson of the importance of self-love and self-acceptance. All of my life I had catered to the perceived demands of those I loved and cared for. I was devastated when many of those people began to leave my life without explanation. An ex-husband with whom I thought I had a strong friendship, a spiritual mentor of over fourteen years, my dear niece, and others simply disappeared, discontinued returning my calls, refused to provide even a sentence explaining their decisions to either end or completely alter our relationships. I cried, beat myself up for every mistake I'd made in our interactions, and brainstormed ways to get these people back in my life or, at the very least, to just talk to me.

None of this worked. What did work was realizing my inherent value as a person, a friend, and a family member. What also worked was forgiving myself for any mistakes I'd made in the past and accepting that the time we had, had come to an end. I had to spiritually release the people I loved forever and leave it to the universe to work it out. My peace returned. Forgiving myself helped me heal from the losses. The universe brought new spiritual teachers into my life and others who had the ability to resolve differences and express hurt in a healthy manner. This was water to my soul. If I'd held on to the past, I would have continued being hurt and damaged by others' treatment of me. I found peace with one of them, although that peace looked nothing like what I expected or hoped it would. However, that peace was divinely perfect.

I participated in a "rite of passage" ritual when I turned forty. It was a wonderful celebration of my womanhood that grounded me in the grace of midlife and the joys it can bring. My ceremony included participation in a Native American sweat lodge ritual, drumming and poetry activities, and a visit to my favorite spa. Midlife is one of the most spiritual stages in life, depending on how we perceive it. The culmination of life lessons, the incorporation of revelations, and the shedding of the old in order to embrace the new make every year a dance of love, empowerment, and healing. What an honor to be a part of the midlife circle! Ase'.

4

In Search of Satisfaction

Romance and Sexuality

*I'm finding that as I go through different phases of my womanhood,
I learn new and different things about myself emotionally, physically, and sexually. For example, when I was younger I wanted to be
chosen; it was important for guys to see me as sexually attractive. As
an adult I'm discovering that it's more important for me to define my
own sense of my sexual attractiveness.*

— Julia A. Boyd, Embracing the Fire: Sisters
Talk about Sex and Relationships

A sly glance. A slow dance. A first kiss. Stolen moments alone together. These are not the sole domains of the young. Older women
also know the sweetness of new love. Or the joys of loving someone for the better part of a lifetime. Just because we are getting
older doesn't mean we don't feel longing or desire. Passion and romantic love can be important parts of our lives always.

Indeed, for some, midlife is the sexual prime of life. Many
women blossom during their middle years and feel more sensual
than ever before. Because of menopause, certain women feel released from fears of unwanted pregnancy and therefore have more
intense sexual experiences. After years of attending to the needs of
children, some may have new time to engage in leisurely lovemaking with their partners. For others, it may have taken until
midlife to truly know what makes them feel good in bed. Still oth-

ers may feel more confident exploring their desires or may become more aware of their sexual preferences. Whatever the reason, many sisters don't call older age "ripe" for nothing.

However, midlife also can bring physical changes—menopause, hysterectomy, or illness—that can make sex less pleasing. Women in this situation may face concerns about their femininity, mourn the loss of their libido, and worry how these changes will affect their relationships. They may be challenged to find strength in the midst of difficulty until they are able to rediscover their sense of themselves as whole and complete women, no matter what.

Other women may become less interested in sex and romance for different reasons. They've "been there, done that" and have moved on to more intriguing pursuits. These women may find their greatest longing is to sing arias, start a business, learn French, run a soup kitchen, write a novel, take up belly dancing, or travel to exotic locales. For these sisters, sharing their lives and their beds with a good lover is just the icing on an already satisfying cake.

At midlife, we continue to define who we are, spiritually, socially, professionally, emotionally, intellectually, and sexually. And we may be surprised at our new definitions.

Age and Sexuality

MAYA ANGELOU

My husband was a man, my son a boy, so I accepted that it was my husband's right and responsibility to speak to our five-year-old son about sex. However, it didn't happen that way.

Guy came home from school one afternoon and asked me if I knew where babies come from. I admitted I did know. There was an "I bet you don't" look on his face and a "Got you this time" cockiness in his stance.

"Well, from where, then?" he asked.

This was not the moment to fudge or hesitate, and certainly not the time to say, "Your father will tell you when he comes home."

I said, "Babies come from the mother's body."

He was crestfallen.

"How long have you known that?"

"For a long time."

"Well, why didn't somebody tell me?"

"I guess because you never asked before."

His interest seemed to ebb, and I offered him a glass of milk. I breathed deeply in relief as he drank.

He put the glass down on the counter and asked, "Do you know how the baby got in the mother's stomach?"

I had relaxed too soon. There was no slyness on his face. This time he was just a genuinely curious five-year-old. Again time had caught me in its clutch. I decided to be very matter-of-fact about the matter.

I reminded him of the names of his private parts.

He nodded.

I said, "Well, when a couple wants a baby the man puts his penis into the woman's vagina and he deposits a sperm and the sperm meets the mother's egg and they grow together and after nine months the baby comes out."

Guy's face was scrambled into a mask of distaste. "Dad did that to you? Wow. You really must have wanted a baby bad."

"I wanted you."

"Wow. I'm glad you didn't want any more . . . or he'd be doing that all the time. Wow!"

Disgust took him out of the room, his small head wagging in puzzlement.

Alas, I have seen that same revulsion on children's faces when there is the slightest hint that their parents might be having sex. The extraordinary element in this account is that the children are in their thirties, forties, and fifties.

An African American woman I know had parents who were married for forty years. The father had a lingering and painful illness during which the mother was his devoted and usually cheerful attendant. The father died. Three years later my acquaintance severed relations with her mother. The mother had dared to take up with a gentleman friend. The daughter, who is thirty-five years old and twice divorced, was repelled by the thought that her mother was being intimate with a man, and displeasure stretched beyond her control.

A group of friends and acquaintances met after church at a hotel for Sunday brunch. The unhappy woman let her horror over her mother's friend take control of the conversation.

"What could they possibly be doing together? She's nearly sixty and he's got to be sixty-five. Can you imagine them naked together? All that wrinkled skin rubbing against the other?"

Her face was an ugly mask. She puckered and pouted and sulked.

"Old people shouldn't have sex. Just thinking about that turns my stomach."

Sitting at the table were black women, whose ages ranged from seventy to seventeen. There was silence for a moment after the tirade, then almost everyone began to speak at once.

"Are you crazy?"

"What's wrong with you?"

"Old folks don't have sex? Who told you that lie?"

One woman waited until the clamor had subsided and asked sweetly, "What do you think your momma and daddy did after you were born? They stopped doing the do?"

The whiner answered petulantly, "You don't have to be nasty." The statement brought howls of derision.

"Girl, you are sick."

"Get a grip."

And the oldest lady in the room said, "Honey, tired don't mean lazy, and every good-bye ain't gone."

I was reminded of my mother when she was seventy-four. She lived in California with my fourth stepfather, her great love, who was recovering from a mild stroke. Her telephone voice clearly told me how upset she was. "Baby. Baby, I've waited as long as I could before bothering you. But things have gone on too long. Much too long."

I made my voice as soft as hers had been hard. "Mom, what's the matter? I'll take care of it." Although I lived in North Carolina, I felt as close as the telephone, airlines, and credit cards allowed me to be.

"It's your poppa. If you don't talk to him, I'm going to put his butt out. Out of this house. I'll put his butt on the street."

This last husband of Mom's was my favorite. We were made for each other. He had never had a daughter and I had not known a father's care, advice, and protection since my teens.

"What did Poppa do, Mom? What is he doing?"

"Nothing. Nothing. That's it. He's not doing a damn thing."

"But, Mom, his stroke."

"I know. He thinks that if he has sex, he'll bring on another stroke. The doctor already told him that isn't true. And I got so mad when he said he might die having sex, that I told him there's no better way to go."

That was funny, but I knew better than to laugh.

"What can I do, Mom? Really, I mean there is nothing I can do."

"Yes, you can. You talk to him. He'll listen to you. Either you talk to him or I'll put him out on the street. I'm a woman, I'm not a damn rock."

I knew that voice very well. I knew that she had reached her level of frustration. She was ready to act.

I said, "OK, Mom. I don't know what I will say, but I'll talk to Poppa."

"You'd better do it soon, then."

"Mom, you leave the house at five-thirty this evening, and I'll telephone Poppa after you leave. Calm your heart, Mom, I'll do my best."

"OK, baby, 'bye. I'll talk to you tomorrow."

She was not happy, but at least she had calmed down. I pondered throughout the day and at six o'clock California time I telephoned.

"Hi, Poppa. How are you?"

"Hey, baby. How you doing?" He was happy to hear my voice.

"Fine, Poppa. Please let me speak to Mom."

"Oh, baby, she left here 'bout a half hour ago. Gone over to her cousin's."

"Well, Poppa, I'm worried about her and her appetite. She didn't eat today, did she?"

"Yes, she did. Cooked crab cakes and a slaw and asparagus. We ate it all."

"Well, she's not drinking, is she?"

"She had a beer with me, and you can bet she's got a Dewar's White Label in her hand right now."

"But, Poppa, something must be wrong. I mean, is she playing music and cards and things?"

"We played Take 6 all day on this music system you sent us, and I know she's playing dominoes over there with your cousin Mary."

"Well, Poppa, you seem to think her appetite is strong."

"Oh, yeah, baby, your momma got a good appetite."

"That's true, Poppa." I lowered my voice. "All her appetites are strong. Poppa, please excuse me—but I'm the only one to speak to you—but it's true her love appetite is strong, too, and, Poppa, please excuse me, but if you don't take care of her in that department, she will starve to death, Poppa." I heard him cough, sputter, and clear his throat.

"Please excuse me, Poppa, but someone is at my door. I love you, Poppa."

There was a very weak, "Bye, baby."

My face was burning. I made a drink for myself. I had done the best I could, and I hoped it would work.

The next morning, about 7:00 A.M. California time, my mother's voice gave me the result.

"Hi, darling, Mother's baby. You are the sweetest girl in the world. Mother just adores you." She cooed and crooned, and I laughed for her pleasure.

Parents who tell their offspring that sex is an act performed only for procreation do everyone a serious disservice. With absolute distress, I must say that my mom died four years after that incident, but she remains my ideal. Now in my sixties, I plan to continue to be like her when I reach my seventies, and beyond, if I'm lucky.

Trust Me

PEARL CLEAGE

"OH-H-H-H-H-H!"

The intensity of the orgasm shook me awake and I called his name out loud. "Mitch!"

Once my heart slowed down, I looked at the clock—five-thirty. The sun wasn't even up yet. Plenty of time for a fast forty winks. I pulled the covers over my head to see if I could will myself back to sleep and was hit full blast by the loamy smell of my own pleasure. *Sweet Mitch.*

This was a good sign. He always comes to me like this when I'm getting ready to do something really important. Sort of like a kiss for luck. It's not the only time I dream about him, but it's the only time the dreams are X-rated. I don't know why. I don't try to conjure him up this way, but I don't kick him out of bed either.

I used to feel guilty about it and then one day I thought, well, hell, if the widow can't ease her permanent heartache by self-pleasuring in her sleep to dreams of her late husband, then what's the poor woman to do? It's not like I took a vow of celibacy or anything. It's just that Idlewild is a very small town and all the men are old enough to be my father or young enough to be my son, or they used to go fishing with my husband and trying to date me just makes them miss him more. So, I make do with the memories and a little self-pleasuring every now and then.

I think *self-pleasuring* sounds infinitely sexier than *masturbation.* I got the term from one of Sister Judith's books. It had a whole chapter on sacred self-pleasuring rituals, featuring photographs and testimonials gathered from what the book described as "active women's collectives throughout Northern California." Personally,

I don't think everything needs its own ritual, but these women are living in the Bay Area. Rituals are their life.

By now, I'm pretty much resigned to the way things are, but sometimes when I think about the fact that I'm only forty-something and there is a very real possibility that I might never make love again, *I can't breathe.* But just for a minute, then I'm OK.

I might as well get up. It was going to be a long day. I had to drive over to the state capital and try to buttonhole enough bored politicians to make sure they vote to fund the proposal I'd spent the last three months of my life working on. I knew it was a long shot. They think the girls in my program are a bunch of wild women whose insanity does not deserve the support of Michigan's hardworking taxpayers, but I've seen the changes these girls can make in their lives once they have a working definition of what it means to be a *free woman*, and that's the whole point, right?

This is one of those moments when I really miss my sister, Ava. She did a lot of fund-raising with me, but she and her husband, Eddie, are spending the next couple of months traveling around the country in a little camper. They got it from one of the old guys up here who hadn't used it in years but who couldn't stop talking about the good times he had with his wife when they drove it to California every summer *back in the day.*

My daughter, Imani, went with them. I miss her a lot, but Ava and Eddie are her parents as much as I am, even if my name is the only one on the adoption papers, and they wanted to take her as much as she wanted to go. I'm flying out to meet them when they get to San Francisco, and we'll all drive back together. Hopefully, by that time, I'll have raised the rest of the money we need to keep my program open, but *from where?*

Sister Judith would probably remind me that the beginning of doubt is the end of faith. I hate it when she says stuff like that.

There's something about her *certainty* that makes me want to argue even when I agree. Plus, discussions of faith always make me nervous. Not that I'm cynical. Just realistic.

Here's what I believe: life is much harder than anybody can possibly tell you, but it doesn't matter because even if they could, you wouldn't believe them and what good would it do anyway? You've still got to get up in the morning and figure out how to spend the next sixteen or seventeen hours before you can legitimately go back to bed, pull the covers over your head, and rest up for the next round, which is what I was busy doing when Mitch woke me up with the memories.

Not that I'm complaining. *No way.* There are a lot worse ways to greet the day than being warmed by memories of the sweetest love you ever had. *Trust me.*

Gray Pussy Hair

OPAL PALMER ADISA

my girl-friend
calls me up distressed

she has spotted
her first gray pussy hair

what am i going
to do she laments

dye the top
and pluck the bottom

i advise

and no more doing it
with the lights on

Safer Sex (before and) after Fifty

GALE MADYUN

I work with seniors, so the reality of people engaging in sexual activity well into their eighties was not a surprise to me. But the breakdown in information for middle-aged women and those older to engage in safe, healthy sexual relationships after being widowed, divorced, or simply single was brought home to me not long ago. I was talking with a seventy-nine-year-old relative about my activism around HIV/AIDS and sexual health. She froze and with a look of horror asked, "Oh, my God, can I get it?" Then she confided that she often had unprotected sex with a longtime companion and that she knew he had relations with another woman friend. In fact, she herself had another male friend with whom she was occasionally intimate.

And I knew from personal experience that unprotected sex—no matter how old the partners—could lead to a sexually transmitted disease (STD): a few years ago, when I was fifty, I learned that my lover of three years had given me one. I was dumbfounded, and besides the emotional pain it generated, my own trusted physician, in a misguided effort to comfort me, told me the STD was not necessarily the result of my partner's betrayal. The visit to the physician was just a confirmation for me that something was wrong. My partner and I had already discussed the dissolution of the relationship. I was stunned when he told me that as far as he could tell I had everything I wanted in the relationship. The pain of someone feeling trapped in a relationship with me was very difficult. Now, in hindsight, the truth of the matter is that we had grown apart and, after three years, we found ourselves not mature enough to dissolve it. With today's diseases, we don't have the luxury to behave as adolescents. I gave him his supply of antibiotics and have not seen him since.

I began to talk frankly with women my age and older about my predicament and heard story after story of mature women who had been infected by husbands or otherwise reliable partners who had sexual contacts on the side. This was my wake-up call.

I realized then that the only person in this world whose sexual behavior I could be absolutely certain about—the only person whose sexual behavior I could *control*—was me! When I was younger, unwanted pregnancy was the big fear, and menopause freed me from that concern. But here I was discovering later in life that I needed to pay closer attention to more current sexual-health information so I could make better choices about taking care of myself.

The statistics about the spread of HIV/AIDS in black communities here and around the world is sobering. The social worker in me was awakened and the sixties activist mentality was renewed for a grassroots sexual-education campaign. As I shared my own hard-won knowledge about sexual health with other women, I became more empowered to speak out about the need for peer education and girlfriend-to-girlfriend conversations to advocate the sexual education of older women to protect themselves. Although the use of latex condoms can reduce the transmission of STDs, HIV, and hepatitis B, many people fifty and older still believe they do not need to use them. They often say there is no reason to change their behavior since they are still fine and healthy after never before using protection in each and every sexual encounter.

This attitude has contributed to a startling statistic: the U.S. Centers for Disease Control and Prevention says that between 1991 and 1996 HIV infections transmitted through heterosexual sex increased by 94 percent in men fifty and older and 106 percent in women fifty and older. Although the numbers of AIDS cases among seniors is relatively small—1,400 in 1996, up from 700 in 1991—experts believe these figures probably underestimate the problem because older people are less likely to be tested for HIV than younger adults. The symptoms of the disease may even be masked by other health problems or simply attributed to aging. Consequently, one of this country's fastest-growing HIV demographic groups is heterosexuals age fifty and older.

Though we associate sexual vitality almost exclusively with youth, the good news is the drive and desire for sexual intimacy can last far into our eighties. But there is no need to put our health at risk. We should be tested to be sure about our present HIV status and then be prepared to require that all future sexual encounters happen with the correct use of a latex condom.

So, what if you have never consistently used condoms before? Whatever happened to growing wiser as you grow older? These days the pharmaceutical industry celebrates its ability to assist people infected with HIV/AIDS to maintain and extend their lives. But the real triumph over HIV/AIDS may not be just developing a successful treatment or cure. The real triumph will come when all of us have the information and the personal self-respect to embrace the tools of prevention—the consistent, correct use of condoms by sexually active people, no matter how old we are.

Plum Jelly in Hot Shiny Jars

AKASHA GLORIA HULL

It was the regret of her life. Aunt Winnie raged, lying on the damp straw mattress, unable to sleep, unable to shut off the anger as her brain pulsed and careened through the past. Many heinous scenes blasted her eyes, many things she had wanted or not done. But in the end, it was this one, halfway-opened promise that tore her apart. *I wish I had whirled like a madwoman, thrown my good name to the dogs. I wish I had reared up and roared myself blind. I wish, oh, I wish I had grabbed the bauble the devil dangled in front of me and pulled it hungrily into my mouth like a bright teething toy. Maybe, then, I wouldn't be dying in this early old age, harboring a grudge against God, rusty blood leaking like a guilt-pointing finger from my unfulfilled womb.*

She rolled over on her other side, slightly lifting her body, twisting her rumpled nightgown straight across her hips, then settling back down—feeling once again the orange waves of memory that would not let her rest.

She had been going on fifty. It was 1838. Mantu had just turned twenty when he showed up at their door the first of June. Her husband, Joshua, had told her about him—the son he had never been close with, now living two plantations southeast of them in Beaufort County. But she had not laid eyes on Mantu. And though she was expecting him, when he finally arrived, the sight of so much vibrant male beauty nearly rendered her blind. He stood there with a bundle of clothes on his back and his long, strong hands and straight, squared shoulders weighed with tools, ready to fix, build, or fabricate whatever Master Clayton wanted for the six lavish months he had bought out his skilled carpenter time.

Winnie wanted to say, "Hi, how you do?" but the greeting was stuck somewhere between the sudden upbeat of her heart and the vacuum her last departing breath had left in her throat. There was no air with which to strum, good thing, for the melody she might have played would have given her away. She was supposed, she thought, to stepmother this boy, but she wanted to grin like a girl, pull him into the house, and set off dancing.

Instead, she reached for one of the burlap sacks in his hands as he said, "Aunt Winnie, mother Winnie. I'm Mantu." His voice was a slow, clear line that hung between them. She still couldn't take hold of anything but the sack of tools, heavier than she had imagined.

Stepping away from the entrance, she let him through the door. The half-confident, half-uncertain shine in his dark, sloe eyes helped her to find her tongue.

"I'm glad to see you. I'm happy that you came." Her voice pitched low, the vowels broad and open. Everything she didn't mean to say vibrated beneath her strangely appropriate words.

"Joshua said I could stay here with you all. But if it's not easy convenient, I can put up in the quarters," Mantu rushed back his response, even as he allowed his gaze to roam slowly over her face and the neat, crowded room around them.

"No, please. There's space here for you. I want you to stay. Please, come on in." It was an odd exchange. He seemed to have been asking her another, bigger question, like more than nights of comfortable sleep depended upon it. She was answering that question with the fresh truthfulness of a blossoming girl who hadn't yet learned how to flirt. Her heart and her blood were singing. Her mind didn't know what to do with itself.

From that moment on, Aunt Winnie split in two. The self everybody saw went right on tending and taking care. She skillfully slave-mistressed the busy South Carolina plantation, holding the reins even more responsibly whenever Miz Katie got gripped by one of her fits. She also kept being a good wife to her good husband, the steady manservant she had taken up with around the time young Miss was born the flood year of '23, when they were both in their mature mid-thirties. That good woman self of her managed to stay intact. But, from the very outset, a young flower-pink girl, the good woman's shadow, sat down at the table with Mantu and presented herself like a warm flickering light.

"There's greens left over from last night's supper. Can I get you some?"

Mantu accepted them and asked her, wasn't she hungry, too? and have a few with him. He unrolled a waxed cloth and added cold cornbread from his pack to their impromptu meal.

"I made this bread," he told her. She was chewing with more deliberation than usual after nibbling a coarse, crumby bite.

"There's something you put in here that's giving it a different taste." She was trying to place the faintly sweet, slightly herby flavor.

"Guess," he said.

"I can't guess what I don't know. Everything I think of, I know that's not it. So, it don't make no sense for me to call that out."

He was sort of puzzling at her. However, all he said was, "Very tasty greens."

"Thank you. I make the best greens of anybody on the place."

He took what she said for a challenge. "You should try mine."

"How do you cook 'em?" Winnie asked.

"With red pepper, lots of onion and garlic, a few plum-ey tomatoes, and a thing or two else I decide." He kept his beautiful face thrust forward, fork momentarily suspended, waiting for her reply.

"That's how I do mine, too," she said.

"I guess that's how come I like 'em." He settled back in his seat, scooping up another fork full, the double tines of the old silver utensil disappearing in his smiling wide mouth.

The Aunt Winnie part of her intruded to marvel that she was sitting here contented as a goose swapping recipes for greens with this self-possessed boy. Her shadow kept right on dancing.

"Who taught you how to cook?"

"My m'am. She died three years ago. I could pick up cooking just as quick as I learned how to build things. People try to stop me. They say I ought to spend my time doing what other folks can't. But I still keep right on cooking. It's something I love to do."

She wanted to ask him what else he loved, but kept that question for another time and place.

"I think it's nice you know how to cook." She sounded as lilting as spring, a flute-like timbre floating on top of her usual rich, brothy bass.

Mantu sat easy, composed, in the chair in front of her, the midafternoon brightness splaying all around him, his wild hair thick and waving every which way on his head. Through the narrow window, she could see the pinkish-red and green plums on the finicky plum tree beside the cabin. Her mind drifted. She saw Mantu winding gracefully among the rough, irregular branches, picking the plums when both of their hemispheres turned ripe red. She saw herself sweating as she boiled the jelly. She saw him carefully rinsing jars in a scalding hot kettle of water. She saw the deep-dyed jelly staining the air outside its shiny clear jars. She saw herself and Mantu, linked, arms about each other, enjoying the sight. Then she came back into herself.

There was nothing that needed saying. They were eating greens and cornbread as if it were a ceremony. A trine of lovely quiet fire flowed through and around them. She had never experienced such joy with another person. A subtly radiant girl—if anyone took the time to look at her—she had been traded and mated, mated and traded again and again, until each master gave up on her breeding potential, some of them after strenuously trying themselves. A few of the men she was paired with she had liked well enough to learn what could be good about sex—but without opportunity to fully open either her body or heart. As she matured, black men and white—like the itinerant dry goods peddler—were still attracted to her and, like the funny little peddler, tried to draw her out of the self-sufficient shell that she and her life had gradually erected around her. It didn't happen, had not happened even with Joshua.

But now, eyes swimming with Mantu, she could have happily sat where she was for the rest of her life. He felt as sweet and familiar as a tenderly diapered infant, yet as thrilling a lover as any woman would want the man at her bosom to be. Within his hot ring of youth and vitality, her own pure, powerful being awakened, a force like she had never, ever felt before.

Bliss and torment, bliss and torment. High lights of heaven, dark fire of hell. Aunt Winnie turned again in her miserable bed, back facing the wall, remembering one particular plummet of pain. She had gone to the harvest dance knowing she would see Mantu. The day before, he had knocked off work on the rose arbor benches and called to her, "See you at the dance." It wasn't a date, he was not her beau—but his words gladdened her heart all the same. She had gone to the dance, hoping for she didn't know what to hope for. But something. Something that the young pink girl thought she was going to get. Something that her old self was so disappointed about when it didn't come that she fled the square and went crying off into the anguished woods, salt bitter tears burning her eyes, stinging her cheeks—"why? why? why?— what? why?" welling out of her.

Unbearable images of the lithe, slim, flat-bellied, melon-breasted girls in an assortment of colors catching Mantu's eye and taunting him, "Man-boy. Man-boy. Is that how you call your name?" Wishing on the stars falling all around her for her own nice womanly ripeness to be thirty years younger, experience intact in a smooth new body that he could see suiting his own and able to ring out to him, drawing him frankly in, not having to survive on fevered dreams and casual touches. *My skin is still firm, my knit frame shapely. My breasts in your mouth will taste sweet. There is fragrance enough still flowing between my legs to river your strong pole in.* Winnie's eyes had been raw when she finally stoppered the hot tears and opened them to the warm night air, deciding roughly that the sight of trees lolling above her was better than the heartbreaking pictures parading behind her lids. "Oh, God, dear God, what, tell me, what am I supposed to do?!"

She never found out what Mantu knew about how she felt about him. She could never exactly tell how he felt about her. While her young girl self let the excitement of him wave glistening through her, Aunt Winnie, upright, responsible woman, maintained a safe enough road in which she could walk. She allowed the double parts of her to come together just often enough to see Mantu forget about Winnie the elder-mother and act on what he sensed guiding him from the fire trine and the giddy girl. She knew he enjoyed being with her. She suspected that how he felt when their pleasure flowed easily raised confusion in his mind. Once, speaking out of both of her mouths, she had said there were pleasant things she would like to do with him, did he have the time?

His unresisting eyes smiled, but his voice didn't answer. Her asking had been pulled willy-nilly out of her by the suction force of him spread lazily against a majestic pine tree. For the longest time, she hadn't been able to speak a word, struck dumb again like the very first time she saw him. He was the most beautiful thing on the face of the earth. She was taking in the peculiar hue of his creamy smooth skin, a light-brown, deep-rich mud still mulatto enough to color faintly with bluish blood when a cold made him blow his perfectly shaped nose. She could never exactly call its shade into memory being. When he shifted against the tree, the whole front of him open, his long arms linked and stretching as he cracked his knuckles and threw back his princely head, Winnie had to ask if she could have even a tiny portion. The only other alternative would have been throwing her outrageously agitated body into his startled arms, and who knows, Lord knows, what might have come out of her then. She was doing all she could to keep the narrow road halfway safe for them to walk on. She wished she knew what he knew of the slippery danger. His knowing would have freed her up. His ambiguous innocence protected him. Protected them.

But protection was not what I needed, Aunt Winnie protested, thrashing and furious on her mattress. *I needed to roll in the hay with him, slide on top of his manliness wherever he made his bed. I needed to fit my swollen straight lips to the pointed curve his bass mouth made. I wanted to boom lightning with him in the midst of summer rainstorms, strike fires that consumed nothing but our naked selves.*

In her happy, good moods, Winnie laughed and talked with Mantu through a silently running refrain: "If I were even twenty years younger, or you just twenty years older, there's no way in hell your behind wouldn't belong to me." She thought this with an almost religious fierceness. She had never felt such a knowing that something ought, just simply ought to be.

Soon after his arrival, Mantu had moved down in the quarters. They never discussed that, either. Him bunking in one corner of the front room didn't bother her or Joshua behind the closed curtain of their second room in the back. From the time she and Joshua joined up with each other, their relationship had been more of a sensible partnership than a passionate union. Sexual nights happened only occasionally, not just because he traveled a great deal for the master, but because that had always been their way. The calm, caring manner in which they made love with each other satisfied their bodies' needs. Generally, though, not so much as a swiftly rustling bed sheet, let alone loud grunts and cries, would have given them away. However, alone, in the room by herself when Joshua was gone, so temptingly close to Mantu, Winnie struggled to hold her desiring thoughts in check. But she could not contain the greedy dreams that broke out of her head. After Mantu moved, with or without Joshua beside her, she kept her turbulent longing locked deep within until absolute dead of night.

Winnie never really talked about Mantu either, with Joshua or anyone else. Her idea of what passed between them remained a better secret that way. Like when he showed her a palm full of round shiny pebbles he had gathered on his way to get her opinion about where to position some just-finished cupboard shelves. He had held the pebbles up one by one with long-fingered precision, each stone made special because he was looking so appreciatively at it or maybe because he was bringing the small heap to her.

In early November, Mantu came and ate supper with her when Joshua was away with Ethan, young master of the plantation, visiting friends and buying tailoring cloth. He was baby-clean and handsome in a fresh flannel shirt and newly washed pair of pants. As she reached around him to set his plate on the table, she almost stroked his cheekbone and sucked his ear. Instead, she asked him how his work for Mas' Clayton was going.

"I'm near 'bout done. He wants me to build another storehouse like that first one I put up, and old Miss is trying to get a few more everyday chairs out of me. 'Sides of that and maybe some little projects, I'm just about finished over here."

"So, your time's drawing to a close." Winnie said it, but she didn't like the sound of the words.

"Yep. Looks that way." A long silence—which he broke. "I want to do some more traveling further north and west. Master loves the money I'm bringing in, even without what he don't know I'm holding on to for myself. So—I think he'll keep hiring me out. I'll stay there over Christmas, and maybe the first of the year, I'll be gone again. I want to see more of the country."

You deserve to see the world, Aunt Winnie thought. But she kept that sentiment to herself, feeling like a mother who was alternately lengthening and drawing in her apron strings. No children had actually ever passed out of her body—she was childless—but she knew that tug-of-war.

They talked about the country—Northerners trying to write against slavery, Cherokee Indians forced over into frontier territory. And his badly run home plantation. The world. And then, finally, a little bit about girls. He brought up that subject.

"And I guess sooner or later, I'll get serious with a girl."

"I can't understand why you haven't been already."

"I'm kinda slow, they say. I didn't start growing 'til I turned fifteen. Then I shot up a foot-and-a-half in one summer."

Winnie laughed at the exaggeration, as he continued. "The first time I kissed anybody I was seventeen, at harvest time. I was too busy learning my trade. The big men let me stay with them, so I thought I was pretty important." Mantu sort of puffed up with his young man bigness. "Gals didn't bother with me. Women neither." He kept his gaze level. "But that all's changing now."

It was one of those moments Aunt Winnie didn't know how to handle. The chicken in her won out and she let it pass. Afterward, she asked herself over and over, "Was he hinting at me? Was he warning me off, or egging me on?" At this point, in the middle of this hellish night without end, it felt like a question for the ages.

After supper was over and their talk had grown long, Mantu said he should head home for the night. Whenever they had been together and then they parted, he always hugged her—wide-armed bear hugs that pinioned her fast. In the beginning, she would pull away when she thought the hugs should be over. Somewhere in the middle of their togetherness, he had stopped letting her go, holding her mooshed up against him but with her unable to position the two of them in any more subtle contact. So gripped, one time she had whimpered, little sounds of pent-up emotion that escaped from inside her. When they separated, Mantu's face looked as flushed and awry as her full and twisted heart. It was a while after that before she saw him again.

This supper evening, walking to the door, he had dropped his arm around her shoulder. Winnie's left arm crossed his waist at the back and her right wrapped around his stomach. The ripples of his narrow torso branded the flesh inside her arm, as the cobra image seared itself behind her eyelids. She knew exactly what his chest and belly would look like if she took off his shirt. But she didn't, and he didn't. He hugged her sideways as they stood and said, "Sleep tight."

No sleep at all was coming to her this night. At least, on that last evening when she had been so close to him, she had let herself dream—extravagant and loving meetings between them, silent passion, noisy confessions—anything she could conjure that would fill up the spaces his leaving had left.

She saw less and less of him—even in passing—as his time grew shorter and his list of final tasks kept getting longer. Winnie couldn't believe that, in the end, she found herself saying good-bye to Mantu with a flock of people, all of them poised in the frost-dusted road, hands lifting to the sky. She couldn't believe he was gone, poof, just like that, away from her. She couldn't believe that here, almost five years later, the pain of him still cut her so deep. He was a gift of love, plain and simple. For whatever reason, heaven opened and smiled. Accepting that, she may have been happy. Wanting more than just looks at the pie on the table brought torment to her breast. Thinking about him still was more than her spirit could bear. Damn. Damn. She should have taken him to her. She should have followed the fire, wherever it led.

It Might as Well Be Spring

CARLEEN BRICE

The Cancer Treatment Center had just been remodeled. Nona could tell it was designed to calm a patient's fears. The muted mauves and blues were soothing to the eye and the floors were covered in thick carpet to absorb sound. A large window looked out on a small, currently barren, garden and, on a good day, the mountains far in the background. Nona wondered if people took their treatments outside on the patio when the weather was warm. It was cold and overcast today and the pollution was so bad she couldn't see downtown, let alone the mountains. Apparently, the architects had forgotten about the "brown cloud," the dusty air that hangs over Denver on chilly winter days.

Nona was on her second round of chemotherapy, and she guessed she should feel grateful that it didn't make her so sick anymore. Her doctor said she was doing well, better than he had expected. The tumor hadn't spread any further. But her arms were bruised from IVs, the radiation had burned her chest, nothing tasted good, and she was tired all the time. Tired of all the treatments, tired of slogging back and forth to work through the March snow, and tired of people's advice. Friends and strangers alike felt compelled to tell her to try a macrobiotic diet while they ate from a bag of Cheetos or slurped diet soda with God-only-knows-what kind of chemicals in it. People with bellies hanging over their belts droned on about the healing benefits of yoga. And everyone seemed to have a mother, grandmother, sister, daughter, or best friend who had breast cancer. Folks meant well, she knew, but she was running out of nerves for them to work. And, if all that wasn't bad enough, her new crop of hair had come in partially gray.

Slumped in the chair, she watched the medicine drip out of the plastic bag through the plastic tube into her body and thought, *This is the only juice in my life.*

She closed her eyes and sighed. She missed men. She missed their musty smells and their deep voices. She missed lying in the bed laughing and talking, and, yes Lord, she missed sex, too. It had been almost five years since she was in love, though the only good thing that came out of that relationship was her little girl Sunny. And it had been more than a year since she had slept with anyone. She didn't want to go back to the old days when she went home with any man who suited her for the moment; however, she wouldn't mind someone to go to dinner with or someone to hold her at night when the fear settled in over her with the blankets. But even after almost five years of sobriety, she was too scared to wish for the black woman's holy grail: the good man. Especially now.

She uncrossed and recrossed her legs and reminded herself she had just a few more weeks before it would feel like spring. Crocuses were starting to peek out of the snow, and she had already seen her first robin. She let herself sink into her favorite daydream about what it would be like if she could put together enough money to buy a house. It would be a tiny place on a large lot covered in gardens. She would have a huge vegetable bed with tomatoes, onions, cucumbers, collards, squash, and peppers, and the rest of the land would be covered with any kind of flower that would grow in Denver's arid climate and clay or sandy soil. She opened her eyes. That's what she needed today: something that blossomed with bright colors and sweet smells that would drive the cold out of her bones. Maybe potted carnations or miniature roses.

After treatment, she went to her favorite greenhouse, Urban Flowers. It was expensive, but Nona figured everybody needed a vice, and when she stopped drinking and using drugs, she started spending her money on plants. She walked in the door and inhaled. The air smelled like wet earth and a million blooms. She pushed her cart through the aisles of daffodil, hyacinth, crocus, and tulip bulbs on her way to the indoor plants and stopped at the orchids. She was admiring a delicate yellow-and-brown-speckled blossom when she heard a rich voice with a hint of a southern lilt say, "Looks like it has your name on it."

She looked up and saw a tall man with dark brown skin and salt-and-pepper hair. He was carrying a shopping basket filled with packages of seeds.

"Oh, I don't mess around with these bad boys," she answered.

"Orchids ain't so scary," he said. "Just put 'em in those pots there," he pointed to a display of specially vented clay pots, "and make sure it stays humid around 'em. I got mine in the kitchen, where the air stays moist from cookin' and washin' dishes."

"I have African violets in my kitchen," Nona said.

He grinned. "Kindred spirits."

Nona felt his smile on her skin, raising little bumps on her arms, and she was grateful for the ten pounds she had dropped since she started treatment. She looked at his hands. He wasn't wearing a wedding ring. "What kind of light do they need?"

"I think it depends," he said. "The one I got is like this white one here, and it likes bright sun."

Nona looked at the price tag, fifty-four dollars. "That's a little rich for my blood today."

"They got different ones. Looka here," he picked a smaller plant with tiny pink and purple flowers. "This one is only thirteen," he said. "And they got the soil and pots right here. You should try it."

"Okay," Nona said. She had the feeling she'd be willing to try just about anything he suggested. She picked up the delicate flower and put it in her basket.

"Good!" he said happily.

"I thought I was the only one this crazy about plants," she said.

"Nah, I'm in here all the time."

"Yes, but do you name the plants when you get them home?"

"I'm afraid that's more of a female thang," he chuckled. "But I can't wait to get out in my garden. I'm gonna start some seeds indoors. This snow is 'bout to drive me crazy."

Nona let out a twinkly giggle. She couldn't believe she was flirting, but the way this man filled out his neatly pressed khakis and suede jacket, she sure didn't plan to stop. "Me too. That's why I'm here. I needed something alive and healthy to take home with me," she said, almost blushing at how suggestive she sounded.

"What you planting this year?" he asked.

"Oh, I don't have a garden. I live in an apartment, but my daughter, my oldest daughter who's grown and doesn't even live with me, says it looks like a jungle." *Lord, I'm babbling like I've lost my mind.*

He put his basket down and offered his hand, "My name is Lamont."

"Nona." She shook his hand; it was calloused and cool. "I come here a lot too. Maybe I'll see you again sometime."

"I'm usually here on weekday afternoons. Gets too crowded for me on the weekends."

That's why she hadn't seen him there before. She wondered how he could afford to be buying orchids during the workday. "Do you work nights?" she asked.

"I'm retired."

She was shocked. "Excuse me for being so forward, but either you retired very early or you look really . . ." She didn't want to say "young" because that would make him sound old and she didn't want to say "good" because that would make her sound brazen.

Lamont laughed. "How old do you think I am?"

"Well, I was gonna guess about fifty, but now I don't know," she said.

"I'll be sixty-two in June." He paused, then added, "Now you know you shouldn't be talking to an old man like me."

"That depends," Nona answered. "Are you married?"

His face broke into a relieved smile. "No . . . are you?"

"No, but I do have a four-year-old," she said, thinking she might as well get the subject of Sunny out of the way.

"Well, now it's my turn to be curious, but I know a lady never tells her age. Just tell me you not young enough to be my grand-daughter."

"I'm forty."

"Forty," he whistled. "I was hoping you weren't as young as you looked." He lowered his voice and said, "You know, it's hard to tell with us."

It's these damn gray hairs making him think I was older. Soon as I'm done with chemo, I'm going straight to Belinda's and get my hair colored. "I'm old enough," she said ruefully. "I've also got a twenty-five-year-old."

"I've got a son a year younger than you and a daughter thirty-five," he said, his smile dimming.

What the hell. I am old enough. "Would you like to get a cup of coffee with me sometime?"

He raised his eyebrows and looked around at the flowers. Nona was trying to think of something to say that would bring back his smile when he looked at her and, beaming again, said, "I would like that very much. May I call you?"

His teeth glowed against his dark skin, like light was radiating from him. She wanted to bathe in it. She whipped her business card out of her purse, wrote her home number on the back, and handed it to him.

He looked down at it and said, "Pleased to meet you, Nona Dixon. I'm Lamont Collier. I'll be calling you soon?"

She nodded.

He picked up his basket. "Well, I best be going," he said, staying right where he was.

"Me too," she answered, but she didn't move either. They both laughed.

Finally, he nodded his head. "Good-bye, Miz Dixon."

"Mr. Collier."

He headed toward the checkout line with his basket of seeds. "Come on, Pinkie," Nona said to the orchid and went the other direction toward the rest of the houseplants, though she didn't know why. She wasn't even thinking about flowers anymore. She got what she came for.

The Company She Keeps

COLLEEN McELROY

finally she no longer
worries about the moon
and children   about
the socks missing
in the wash   or the mail
that arrives late
now she refuses to cover
her lust   justly seeks
the most prodigious
outlet   the lover
immune to age who parlays
time into skill
oh she's practiced
running down the beach
into the sea without
worry of drowning
or being pulled
in by undertow
and she's good
at what she does

she no longer cares
if neighbors catch
her in the act
yelling like a banshee
over each conquest
caught in the blaze of a fire she makes
every night where

she is the match
he the flint she lights
she shocks slim hipped
youth who believe they
own all that is delicious
this *flagrante delicto*
this one act she coddles
to perfection
I'm warning you she says:

let me in the door and
I'll take the room   let
me in the room and
I'll claim the house   let
me in the house and
I'll own the block   let
me onto the street and
the town is mine so
best move now cause
I'm landlady here
and you're never
too old to learn

he leans over
dismisses the pain
in his old joints
kisses her toes

from *Do-It-Yourself Rainbows*

J. CALIFORNIA COOPER

Berta cried a little for him. He hadn't been a bad husband. He was in his sixties when he died and she was forty-six. That can be a big difference for a lot of things, but he had been settled and secure. A first for her. Now, he was gone and she was alone.

She'd walk through the little empty house, sadly, and cry some more, cause it was lonely. In time, she began to walk through that little house, sayin, "It's mine. I got a little house, paid for. A little car, furniture and all that, paid for. It's all mine. I guess I am secure." But she was still lonely and she didn't know for what, cause she really didn't miss Spencer, she was just used to another person bein in the house.

Spencer hadn't left her no big insurance or nothin. She did a few jobs of day work a couple days a week and she had his small Social Security check. She had almost always, in the last few years, been able to save her money cause they didn't have no bills. She was alright if she didn't move to the left or the right too far or too fast. You know.

She kept the yard and house up, cause she had been doin it alone for years. She just took to lookin even more thoughtful and starin off into space.

Then, one day she just brought all kinds of things out that house and sat em on the sidewalk. Put a sign out that said, "See something you want, take it. I'm throwin it all away." Now the house was almost empty. She cleaned it up and sat around lookin out in space again.

Soon after that, I visited her like I do, now and again. She was sittin up in her livin room with tears in her eyes. Just sittin.

I ask her, "What's the matter, Berta? You missin Spencer that much? Still?"

She answered and sounded like she was mad a little. "No, I ain't missin Spencer, rest his soul. I'm missin life."

I did understand and I didn't understand. "Life?"

She said, "Life." She looked up at me, tears gone now. "I want to be happy in life sometime. Thrilled. Like . . . that song say; flyin over the rainbow like a bluebird. There ain't never been no rainbows in my life."

I didn't say nothin, cause I knew what she was talkin about and I didn't feel like lyin to make nobody feel better.

She went on, "Spencer was alright. But in the beginnin it was like he was my father. In the end, it was like I was his mother. I didn't hate him, but I didn't love him. He just was a home for me. We ain't made love for years and when he was crawlin up on top of me, it still wasn't nothin cept somethin for him. I ain't never felt nothin in no sex. I know it's somethin to feel, cause love is too popular in this world. And I ain't had none of it. I ain't never had no climax in life and I am forty-six years old and pretty soon I am goin to die. I ain't done nothin but wash, cook, clean, rub and look at TV and read a little."

"Oh, Berta," I started.

"And I hate that name 'Berta,' cause it sounds like a piece of wood! Everything I got is cause somebody else gave it to me. I ain't never picked my life and nothin in it, for myself."

"Oh, Berta, I mean . . ."

"Well, I'm goin to change all that. I'm gonna get me a life of my own. With some love in it! And somebody who's a man, my age. I'm gonna get me a climax. If I have to build my own rainbow, I will."

I nodded my head. "You mean a climax to life like some point in it?"

She nodded her head. "That too! But what I mean is a orgasm. A orgasm." She looked directly at me like she was darin me to disagree or argue with her. "You may think that's nothin, but you been happy with your husband and you all was the same age and you picked him and he picked you. You ain't never looked like you was in misery to me, less it was about money. You ain't never complained bout no lovin. You got your own rainbow."

I smiled, "Well, I . . ."

She said, "Well, I am too."

Over the next few weeks, Berta was buyin things and redoin her house on the inside. I offered her my help, but she said, "No, I'm gonna do this all by myself." And she did.

When it was finished, I went to see it. She had kept the twin beds in the bedroom, but everything else was changed. It was furnished nice, but it was somethin about it like the Arabian Nights lady. And she had incense burnin. Flowin drapes, soft material couch, low tables and such. Soft colors. That little house didn't know what to do with itself!

I told her, "It looks good. Like a woman's house. You really workin on it."

She switched her little behind on by me. "And I ain't through."

When I left her house I was in wonder, but I smiled cause I blive people should build their life like they want to. I passed Ms. Winch, a widow and Berta's closest neighbor, who came out to the gate as I passed.

Ms. Winch smiled and beckoned to me. "Girl, what does her house look like? I seen all that stuff they was bringin in there. That ain't no real spensive stuff, but it ain't cheap either! She spendin that man's money like it was water. You better tell her something! His dyin done made a fool of that woman!"

Now, I don't worry bout what people think, less it's my husband. I just told Ms. Winch, "That man's money is her money too. She is a young woman. She ain't old as me and I ain't old as you. So if she don't do some livin now, when she gonna do it?"

Ms. Winch said, "Well, you a fool too," and went on back in her house her husband left her that was still just like the day he died and left it a long time ago.

Now, I thought about what Ms. Winch said. I realized that I had always thought when a woman got to be round forty, forty-five years old, her life was over, in a way of speakin. She was sposed to be lonely if her husband died and she was that age. But I wasn't so sure that was true. Who has to be alone just cause somebody left or died?

Now, I don't know was it a magazine or the TV gave her the idea, cause she had always done her own hair. But Berta commence to goin to the hairdresser and had her hair cut and styled. Then she started shoppin and dressin different. When I visited her one day, on her beautiful new dresser she had a rack of face creams and such, to get rid of wrinkles and such. She even had some on her face!

Well, I smiled to myself and was glad for her. Hell, be happy doin what you want to do.

Then, one day she jumped out that little car of hers and I looked in her face to say "hello" and Berta had her face made up. And was lookin good! She was gettin a new look! She looked so proud of herself and I was proud for her. Berta looked ten years younger! Well, her life had been slow, so her face wasn't raged with time noway.

I followed her in her house. I liked goin in there, it made me feel . . . different somehow. Like a lady, a woman. And I know I always been one anyway, but this was a different woman. I started to say, "Berta? Girl, you look good!"

She smiled, a happy smile, and said, "My name ain't Berta no more. I got another name. My middle name is Marie and I'm addin a 'La' to it, so now my name is LaMarie." We laughed together and I said, "All right, LaMarie!"

She poured some Dubonnet wine in some pretty little glasses, handed me one and said, "This ain't nothin bad, they use it in church sometime."

We sipped a minute. I don't know why, but I felt like a modern lady.

She spoke first. "You know . . . some of the men from my church done come here to see me. They were nice. Maybe I could'a liked one of em, but they all just remind me of Spencer. I don't intend to make love with Spencer, in no way. The only one who didn't remind me of Spencer, I really did like, but he didn't come back no more. That hurt. I have not tried sex with anybody, so it can't be sex. But he didn't even come back to try to get some. That means there is somethin I didn't have that somebody else has. Well, I got to wonderin what it was."

I took another sip of wine. "Well, there ain't nothin wrong with you, Ber– . . . LaMarie."

She waved her hand at me. "I am makin myself over."

I had to put my two cents in. "My aunt says if you are too easy to get, they don't want you no more."

She poured two more little drinks. "Your aunt got good sense. And that can hurt more, cause you done gave em some and they don't want no more. Lord, ain't people got a lot of ways to be hurt?" She sipped some more. Her eyes were bright and I just knew she had somethin she wanted to say.

She did. "Listen, girl, do you know that 'On the streets' you don't need to look for no man? That they come lookin for you?"

I sat my glass down after I emptied it. "On the streets? What you talkin about? They ain't lookin for you, they lookin for anybody for twenty or thirty minutes! Them are strangers! You don't want no stranger!"

She sat her glass down. "No, I don't. But I been down there in the French Quarter, watchin them women. They don't look too sad."

I butted in. "They don't get paid for lookin sad."

She leaned forward in her fancy chair. "Yes, they look sad, but they don't look lonely."

I poured my own little glass of wine, I needed it. "They some of the loneliest people on the earth. Even their own man don't really want em."

She shook her head. "They get plenty sex."

I said, "Ummm hummm, too much sex. You ain't talkin bout bein' no prostitute at your age. At any age. Are you?"

She sat back, shakin her new-done head. "I just figure if the men go there to see women, they must not have a woman of their own at home. Now . . . one of them men got to be a good man, bout my age, just lost for a while. I might be the one who catches him. I ain't dyin of old age yet, and I figure if I am clean and good. A good Christian woman . . . they'll think of that! Then I will have the love of my life, maybe. And he must like sex, or he wouldn't be there! I ain't never in my life felt a twinge down there. Not even a tweak! I don't think I'm no sex maniac, but I know one thing. I meeeean to see what that stuff is all about and I'm gonna feel somethin," she pointed, "down there fore I die! Now!"

It was my turn. I said, "Them men don't go down there for no love. For no good! They go down there for nookey."

"Well, I got some. I ain't gonna do it with everybody, Retha! I'm gonna be lookin for the ONE I might want to maybe marry."

I shook my head. "Well, if that don't beat all. Goin to the gutter to find a husband! I done heard of everything now! I done heard of all kinds of ways to get a husband, but I ain't never heard of this way! This is dangerous. You could lose your life out there, stead of finding some love. People don't care about killin you out there in them streets. Give me another glass, I'll buy you some more today."

LaMarie got up to pour the wine. "Well, what am I gonna do? I'm not young. And I'm not old. But, I am lonely . . . and this is the way I see to do it."

I went home later, thinkin to myself, "She is a fool. But she won't be out there long. She gonna see ain't nothin out there worth havin. It's disease out there that eat up penicillin, belch and go on bout their dirty death business." I got home to my safe home and locked the door.

Anyway, she went. In the evenins. She would leave her car home, take the bus, get off in the middle of all that stuff and just walk. She always wore a neat dress, a cute hat, white gloves and neat little shoes. She look like she was goin to church. LaMarie, LaMarie.

Love and Other Geometric Shapes

ESSA ÉLAN

my nerves
are still gossiping about his touch

as I awake sacred in his arms,
arise reminded of my beauty,

brought closer to divinity and
truths existent before elements or reason —

so much passion,
at times it scares me —

waking hours cause my reflection
on love with its past and present meanings —

love was everything yet absolutely nothing: a defiant flooding force
with the obedience of rivers surging toward seas,

finite moments encasing infinite possibilities,
a microscope of wrinkles and imperfections —

games of cubed pegs in round holes,
a hypotenuse never equal to anything.
now, I only measure love against itself
and the perpetual line leading back to him.

Some Buddhists believe
square, triangle, and circle are symbolic of life,

isn't the same true for love?

square forms our room, this bed,
and the sheets that warm us,

triangle shapes our dance with passion
moving opposite, adjacent, ever-connected,

circle: my legs enveloping plunging hips,
his lips poised in a perfect O of scant breaths and wonder—

We have created love in our own self-image,
rendered it flawless, made a mess of it,

cornered it, left it open to boundless sky,
but that's all inconsequential.

Age has taught the true matter of this mass.
And the only matter? . . . Love is ours.

Contributors' Biographies

OPAL PALMER ADISA is a literary critic, poet, prose writer, storyteller, and artist. She is author of *Leaf of Life* (Jukebox Press, 2000), *It Begins with Tears* (Heinemann, 1997), and other books. Her writing has appeared in numerous journals in the United States, England, Canada, and Jamaica. She lives in Oakland, California, with her three children.

BRENDA J. ALLEN is an associate professor in the department of communication at the University of Colorado, Denver. She teaches classes and conducts research on social identity in organizations. She also designs and conducts self-empowerment workshops for women.

MAYA ANGELOU is a poet, educator, historian, actress, playwright, civil rights activist, producer, and director, in addition to being author of twelve best-selling books, including *I Know Why the Caged Bird Sings* and *A Song Flung Up to Heaven*. She is the Reynolds Professor of American Studies at Wake Forest University.

TINA McELROY ANSA is author of the novels *Baby of the Family*, *Ugly Ways*, *The Hand I Fan With*, and *You Know Better*. An avid gardener, birder, and amateur naturalist, she is married to Jonee Ansa, a filmmaker. They reside on St. Simons Island, Georgia.

STEPHANIE ROSE BIRD has been a professor at the School of the Art Institute of Chicago since 1986. As a magical-herbalist, she conducts workshops at the Chicago Botanical Gardens and the Infinity Foundation. She is the author of *Down-home Beauty: An Herbal Guide for Women of Color*. Her book *The Hoodoo Handbook: Af-*

rican American Mysticism, Folklore and Spirituality will be published by Llewellyn Worldwide in 2004.

CARLEEN BRICE, editor of *Age Ain't Nothing but a Number: Black Women Explore Midlife,* is author of two nonfiction books: *Walk Tall: Affirmations for People of Color* and *Lead Me Home: An African American's Guide Through the Grief Journey,* and she has written for *Mademoiselle,* the *Chicago Tribune,* the *Denver Post,* and BET.com. She is currently working on her first novel.

PEARL CLEAGE is a playwright, novelist, and contributing writer for *Essence* magazine. She is author of the *New York Times* best-seller *What Looks Like Crazy on an Ordinary Day, Mad at Miles: A Blackwoman's Guide to Truth,* and other books. She is the mother of one daughter, Deignan, and lives in Atlanta with her husband, Zaron W. Burnett Jr.

LUCILLE CLIFTON is author of several award-winning collections of poetry and is a two-time nominee for the Pulitzer Prize.

J. CALIFORNIA COOPER is author of *Homemade Love, In Search of Satisfaction, Some Love, Some Pain, Sometime, The Wake of the Wind,* and other books. The 1989 American Book Award winner lives in northern California.

MIRIAM DeCOSTA-WILLIS is editor of *Blacks in Hispanic Literature, Homespun Images: An Anthology of Black Memphis Writers and Artists* and is coeditor of *Erotique Noire: Black Erotica.* Her articles on Afro-Hispanic and African American literature and history have appeared in such journals as *Callaloo, Latin American Literary Review,* the *West Tennessee Historical Society Papers,* and the *Revista/Review Latinoamericana.*

DIANE DONALDSON is a freelance journalist based in Omaha, Nebraska. She has worked for both the *Omaha Star* and the *Kansas City Star* newspapers and holds a master's degree in communications.

RITA DOVE, U.S. poet laureate from 1993 to 1995, is author of several collections of poems, including *Mother Love* and *On the Bus with Rosa Parks,* as well as the novel *Through the Ivory Gate* and other works.

ESSA ÉLAN is a writer in the Atlanta area whose recent work has been published in *Clean Sheets, Black Venus, Journal Femme, Amoret Online,* and *1stPerson.org.* She also publishes a monthly newsletter, *Essa Élan Online,* which is hosted on Topica.com, and she is currently compiling an anthology of short southern fiction entitled *Scorch.*

MARILYN HUGHES GASTON, M.D., a member of the National Medical Association and the prestigious Institute of Medicine of the National Academy of Sciences, is coauthor of *Prime Time: The African American Woman's Complete Guide to Midlife Health and Wellness.*

NIKKI GIOVANNI has recently published an illustrated "love poem" entitled *Knoxville, Tennessee* for her grandmother, Louvenia Watson. She is also author of *The Selected Poems of Nikki Giovanni* (1996), the children's book *The Genie in the Jar* (with Chris Raschka), and other works. The 1996 winner of the Langston Hughes Award, Dr. Giovanni is a member of the National Advisory Board of the Underground Railroad Freedom Center. In April 2002, she was awarded the first Rosa L. Parks Woman of Courage Award.

JEWELLE GOMEZ is an activist and writer. She's the author of seven books, including three collections of poetry, a book of personal essays, and her black vampire novel, *The Gilda Stories,* a cult favorite since its publication in 1991. She is on the advisory board for the National Center for Lesbian Rights and for the Human Sexuality Archives at Cornell and is currently the director of the Cultural Equity Grants Program for the San Francisco Arts Commission.

TRUDIER HARRIS-LOPEZ is J. Carlyle Sitterson Professor of English at the University of North Carolina, Chapel Hill, where she teaches courses in African American literature and folklore. She is author and editor of more than twenty books, including *Saints, Sinners, Saviors: Strong Black Women in African American Literature. Summer Snow,* her collection of personal essays, is forthcoming from Beacon Press.

JOAN HOPEWELL-HARTGENS, M.S.W., a freelance writer and playwright, has been published extensively throughout the past two decades in national and international publications, including *Glamour, Essence, Class, Channels,* and others. Ms. Hartgens's plays include *Rosemary & Thyme* and the Off-Broadway-produced *Obsidian.* In addition to her writing career, Ms. Hartgens worked as a social worker and placed children with special needs with loving adoptive families. After an eleven-year battle with ovarian cancer, Ms. Hartgens died in November 2002, leaving behind three adult children and eight grandchildren, all of whom are very proud of her many accomplishments.

AKASHA GLORIA HULL published many groundbreaking books and articles during the 1970s and 1980s as a black feminist literary critic. The best known of these include *All the Women Are White, All the Blacks Are Men, But Some of Us Are Brave: Black Women's Studies* (coedited), and *Color, Sex, and Poetry: Three Women Writers of the Harlem Renaissance.* In addition, she is a professor, lecturer, poet, and creative writer now living in northern California. Her most recent book, *Soul Talk: The New Spirituality of African American Women* (Inner Traditions, 2001), has been called by *Publishers Weekly* a "powerful, practical and nourishing gumbo." "Plum Jelly in Hot Shiny Jars" is excerpted from the novel she is currently writing.

Ta'SHIA ASANTI KARADE is an award-winning poet, journalist, fiction writer, and filmmaker. She is also a priestess of Yemoja in the Ifa tradition.

ELAINE LEE is editor of *Go Girl: The Black Woman's Guide to Travel and Adventure* published by Eighth Mountain Press in October 1997. Over six thousand books have been sold to date. She is cohost of the Bay Area's first travel radio show, which airs monthly on KPFA-FM. As a freelance writer who specializes in ethnic and women's travel, she has contributed to the following magazines, webzines, and books: *Heart and Soul*, BET.com, *Maiden Voyages, Essence, Emerge, Black Enterprise, Upscale, Ms., Transitions Abroad, Quarterly Black Review of Books*, and *Beyond L.A. Law*, an anthology compiled by Janet Smith and published by Harcourt Brace in 1998.

GALE MADYUN, a women's health activist, is a chapter president of the Older Women's League in the greater Los Angeles area. She is also a retired state geologist and single parent of three college graduates.

COLLEEN McELROY has published a textbook on speech and language development, six books of poetry, and two collections of short stories, *Jesus and Fat Tuesday* and *Driving Under the Cardboard Pines*.

TERRY McMILLAN is author of the national best-sellers *Mama, Disappearing Acts, Waiting to Exhale, How Stella Got Her Groove Back,* and *A Day Late and a Dollar Short.* She also edited the anthology *Breaking Ice.*

GLORIA NAYLOR is author of *The Women of Brewster Place,* which won the American Book Award for fiction, *Mama Day, Bailey's Café, The Men of Brewster Place,* and other books.

ADA NELRIBI is a poet and part-time instructor at Hunter College's Fatata Institute of Cultural Awareness. Her poems have been published in several journals, including *Lucid Stone, Troubadour,* and *Puerto del Sol.*

GAYLE K. PORTER, PSY.D., is a clinical psychologist. Throughout her thirty years as a health professional, she has won awards from many prestigious organizations, including the Black Mental Health Alliance and the National Association of University Women. She is coauthor of *Prime Time: The African American Woman's Complete Guide to Midlife Health and Wellness.*

PATRICIA RAYBON has written for the *New York Times Magazine, Newsweek, USA Weekend,* the *Rocky Mountain News,* and the *Denver Post.* She is author of *My First White Friend: Confessions on Race, Love, and Forgiveness* and teaches journalism at the University of Colorado, Boulder.

S. PEARL SHARP is author of *Black Women for Beginners,* the poetry volumes *Typing in the Dark* and *Soft Song,* as well as the plays *Dearly Beloved* and *The Sustuhs* (all under Saundra Sharp) and a spoken-word CD, *On the Sharp Side.* She starred in the TV movies *Hollow Image* and *Minstrel Man.* Her work as an independent filmmaker includes *Picking Tribes* and the arts documentaries *Life Is a Saxophone* and *The Healing Passage*.

APRIL SINCLAIR is author of the best-selling novels *Coffee Will Make You Black* and *I Left My Back Door Open*.

ELYSE SINGLETON is an award-winning journalist whose first novel, *This Side of the Sky*, was published by Penguin Putnam in fall 2002.

SHEILA STAINBACK has a distinguished career spanning more than twenty years in broadcast journalism. The Emmy Award–winning journalist joined Court TV as a news anchor in February 2000 and also serves as an adjunct professor of journalism at New York University.

TERRI SUTTON lives in Milwaukee, Wisconsin, where she teaches English and history at Milwaukee Area Technical College.

SUSAN L. TAYLOR is senior vice president and editorial director of *Essence* and author of *In the Spirit* and *Lessons in Living*. In 2002, she was inducted into the American Society of Magazine Editors Hall of Fame.

JAN THOMAS is a former corporate public relations manager who spent almost twenty years working for a local telephone company. She now works in higher education and is an aspiring novelist. Jan lives with her husband and dog in Denver, Colorado.

CARMEN TURNER is a paralegal and has been living in New York City since 1995. She has written a book called "House of Spirit Broken," for which she seeks a publisher.

GLORIA WADE GAYLES is author of *My Soul Is a Witness: African American Women's Spirituality, Rooted Against the Wind: Personal Essays,* and *Pushed Back to Strength: A Black Woman's Journey Home.*

ALICE WALKER won the Pulitzer Prize and the National Book Award for her novel *The Color Purple.* Her many other best-selling novels, collections of short stories, collections of essays, and volumes of poetry include *You Can't Keep a Good Woman Down, Possessing the Secret of Joy,* and *Anything We Love Can Be Saved.* Her books have been translated into more than two dozen languages.

WUANDA M. T. WALLS is an eighth-generation Pennsylvanian who writes from Pennsylvania, Colorado, and places afar. Her work has been published in *A Woman Alone: Travel Tales from Around the Globe, Go Girl: The Black Woman's Guide to Travel and Adventure,* and *Gifts of the Wild.*

JACKIE WARREN-MOORE is a nationally and internationally published poet, playwright, and newspaper columnist. Her work has appeared in *Sisterfire: Black Womanist Fiction & Poetry, Spirit & Flame: An Anthology of Contemporary African American Poetry, Passionate Lives, Writing Our Way Out of the Dark: An Anthology of Childhood Sexual Abuse Survivors,* and various other journals, date books, and calendars. She makes her home in Syracuse, New York.

Editor's Acknowledgments

First and foremost, I'd like to thank the women who so eloquently gave voice to the joys and concerns of the middle years. I am indebted to the authors who gave me permission to publish their original works and to publishers (including the folks at *Essence* magazine) who granted permission to reprint materials that had been published before.

To my family and family-in-law, I'd like to say I love you and am so proud and grateful to be part of you. I dedicate my efforts on this book to my mother, Constance Walls, my stepmother, Sharon Brice, and my "play mama," Lovie Boggess.

I am enormously lucky to have been able to compile this collection while I worked for a woman whose support of me stretched far beyond my expectations and hopes. Carol Gibson, vice president of development for National Jewish Medical and Research Center, has been a godsend to me in my quest to pay my bills and follow my creative heart. I also am thankful for the friendship of my coworkers, including Tanya Lehr, Amber Batson, Maryann Hoffmann, and Jean Maguire.

Many friends and fellow writers offered advice and encouragement from the early stages of this book's genesis up through the time it was birthed, including Trina McGuire, Karen Sbrockey, Elaine Lee, Wuanda Walls, Akasha Hull, and Diane Donaldson.

Gareth Esersky, and the staff at Beacon Press, including Joanne Wyckoff, Brian Halley, Tom Hallock, Pam MacColl, Kathy Daneman, David Coen, and Christina Palaia, greeted this anthology with enthusiasm and treated it with great care, which is all a writer could ever want.

My husband teaches me every day what it is to be an artist and a stellar human being. Dirk, I am most grateful to have you in my life.

A portion of the author's proceeds will be donated to the National Black Women's Health project, a national grassroots organization in Washington, D.C.

Credits

"Journal (February 12, 1987)" from *Living by the Word: Selected Writings, 1973–1987*. Copyright © 1988 by Alice Walker, reprinted by permission of Harcourt, Inc.

From *A Day Late and a Dollar Short* by Terry McMillan. Copyright © 2001 by Terry McMillan. Used by permission of the author and Viking Penguin, a division of Penguin Putnam Inc. Dedicated to the author's mother, Madeline Tillman, "who always knew that age wasn't nothing but a number!"

"The Affirmation" from *My First White Friend* by Patricia Raybon. Copyright © 1996 by Patricia Raybon. Used by permission of Viking Penguin, a division of Penguin Putnam Inc.

"Mattie Michael" from *The Women of Brewster Place* by Gloria Naylor, copyright © 1980, 1982 by Gloria Naylor. Used by permission of Viking Penguin, a division of Penguin Putnam Inc.

From *I Wish I Had a Red Dress* by Pearl Cleage. Copyright © 2001 by Pearl Cleage. Reprinted by permission of HarperCollins Publishers Inc. Avon Books.

Lucille Clifton, "new bones" from *Good Woman: Poems and a Memoir, 1969–1980*. Copyright © 1987 by Lucille Clifton. Reprinted with the permission of BOA Editions, Ltd.

Lucille Clifton, "to my last period" from *Quilting: Poems, 1987–1990*. Copyright © 1991 by Lucille Clifton. Reprinted with the permission of BOA Editions, Ltd.

CREDITS

From *Some Love, Some Pain, Sometime* by J. California Cooper. Copyright © 1995 by J. California Cooper. Used by permission of Doubleday, a division of Random House, Inc.

"Choosing Longevity" from *Lessons in Living* by Susan L. Taylor. Copyright © 1995 by Susan L. Taylor. Used by permission of *Essence* magazine.

From *Even the Stars Look Lonesome* by Maya Angelou. Copyright © 1997 by Maya Angelou. Used by permission of Random House, Inc.

From *I Left My Back Door Open* by April Sinclair. Copyright © 1999 by April Sinclair. Reprinted by permission of Hyperion.

"Used" from *Mother Love* by Rita Dove. Copyright © 1995 by Rita Dove. Used by permission of the author and W. W. Norton & Company, Inc.

"Babies??!!" by Tina McElroy Ansa. Copyright © 2002 by Tina McElroy Ansa. Reprinted by permission of William Morris Agency, Inc., on behalf of the author. All rights reserved.

From *Prime Time: The African American Woman's Complete Guide to Midlife Health and Wellness* by Marilyn Hughes Gaston, M.D., and Gayle K. Porter, Psy.D, copyright © 2001 by Marilyn Hughes Gaston, M.D., and Gayle K. Porter, Psy.D. Used by permission of Ballantine Books, a division of Random House, Inc.

"Age" from *Cotton Candy on a Rainy Day* by Nikki Giovanni. Copyright © 1978 by Nikki Giovanni. Used by permission of the author.

CREDITS

"Who Says an Older Woman Shouldn't Dance?" from *Rooted Against the Wind* by Gloria Wade-Gayles. Copyright © 1996 by Gloria Wade-Gayles. Used by permission of the author.

"Letting Go with Love" by Miriam DeCosta-Willis. Copyright © 1993 by Miriam DeCosta-Willis. Used by permission of the author.

"In the Heat of Shadow" by Jewelle Gomez. Copyright © 1988, 2002 by Jewelle Gomez. Used by permission of the author.

"Safer Sex (before and) after 50" by Gale Madyun. Copyright © 2002 by Gale Madyun. Originally published in *Essence* magazine and used by permission of the author.

"Middle-Age UFO" from *Bone Flames* by Colleen McElroy. Copyright © 1987 by Colleen McElroy. Reprinted by permission of the author.

"Adoption: A Midlife Love Story" by Sheila Stainback. Copyright © 2002 by Sheila Stainback. Originally published in *Essence* magazine and used by permission of the author.

"How to Fly into 50 (Without a Fear of Flying)" by S. Pearl Sharp. Copyright © 1993 by Saundra Sharp. Used by permission of the author. Originally published in *Sisterfire: Black Womanist Fiction and Poetry* edited by Charlotte Watson Sherman, HarperPerennial.

NEW BRUNSWICK FREE PUBLIC LIBRARY

3 9309 00152030 0

810.8092   Age ain't nothing but
AGE   a number.

$14.00

DATE			

BAKER & TAYLOR